EMOTION:
The On/Off Switch
For Learning

by
Priscilla L. Vail

Published by
MODERN LEARNING PRESS
ROSEMONT, NJ

Material on pages 146, 147, 206, and 207 excerpted from
Clear and Lively Writing: Language Games and Activities for Everyone,
copyright © 1981 by Priscilla L. Vail.
Reprinted by permission of Walker and Company,
435 Hudson Street, New York, NY 10014.

Dedication

for
Margaret Mayo-Smith,
mentor, model, and merriment maker,
with love, gratitude, and a large dose of irreverence

Acknowledgements

Endless thanks to my husband, Donald; to our children, Melissa, Polly, Lucia, and Angus; our sons-in-law Norman and Mark; and our grandchildren, Luke, Thomas, Jack, Melissa, Jesse, and Willa. Proofreaders, guinea pigs, and models, they have blessed me by hanging out, being themselves, and providing laughter, examples, and love.

The children I teach in school are always my teachers. I thank the students at Rippowam-Cisqua for the insights they've given so generously on our common journey.

Heartfelt thanks to Bert Shapiro, publisher, and Robert Low, editor, who gave this project their blessing over a cup of tea, who would NOT let me say "finished" to a work still in progress, and who have blessed this endeavor with a vision of what it might be.

P.L.V.
1994

TABLE OF CONTENTS

FOREWORD

"I'm not going to do this," said Marvin. "It looks boring." Instead of scolding him, his teacher said, "Here. I'll show you how to get going." Marvin wasn't bored. He was scared. Fear shuts off learning.

"Amy, you're daydreaming again. You need this information for your project." Amy's thoughts kept drifting to her cat, which had to be put down that morning. Sadness, a silent intruder, dims power.

"Oh, come on, Dad, that's not fair!" shouted Christopher. "I HAVE to go to this hockey practice. You can keep me here all you want to, but you can`t make me memorize. I hate it!" Christopher isn't a rotten kid. He's angry. Anger blows fuses and trips circuit breakers.

"I bet I can figure this out," calls Julia. "Give me time and I'll do it." Julia isn't brilliant. She's confident. She's plugged in.

Whether kids are turned on to learning, turned off by learning, or burned out of learning depends in large measure on their emotional positives and negatives.

Positive emotions turn kids on. We see the lights in their eyes. Their thoughts sparkle. Confidence makes incandescence, glowing from within, casting light about, and illuminating learning.

Fear, passivity, or sadness make opalescence — a surface which can reflect light but not generate it. And, stormy negative emotions cause power outages.

Anger is like a lightning strike in an electrical storm. Discouragement is like a heavy, wet snow weighing down wires and breaking connections. Loneliness, like ice, snaps brittle lines. Pessimism floods across the fields of enterprise, seeping into junction boxes. Learning suffers when power is sporadic.

These emotions and experiences are not new, to be sure. But, the swelling number of children who are dealing with multiples of negatives — and the intensity of situations in which young children find themselves — are creations of our era. These result in misdirection of emotional energy and underpowered learning. And, we cannot afford to ignore their jostling, disruptive, weakening effect on classrooms.

In simpler times, teachers had class sizes of around 15 to 20 students whose predominant stances were optimistic and respectful. Across a teacher's career, there would probably have been the 15 to 20% who were dyslexic, the 10 to 20% who were gifted. There would have been some emotionally disturbed children, as well as those with behavior problems, who were probably more manageable then than now because of the tenor of society.

Although human nature was neither sunnier nor nobler in bygone days, norms of acceptable behaviors were more standardized. Therefore, discipline was more consistent, and the need for common courtesies was taken for granted. Parents and educators established the boundaries together, and kids knew where the limits were.

Schooling was based on clearly articulated, shared expectations. Teachers were in school to teach, kids were in school to learn, parents had more time at home, more support from extended families, less haste, fewer choices, and more certainties.

But, traditional patterns are shattering.

Children coping with the realities of today's living may carry worries, sadness, or experiences around inside them which interfere with their ability to learn. Metaphorically, increasing numbers of children have low-wattage bulbs, frayed cords, damaged plugs, ill-fitting sockets, or tired generators, which make for marginally illuminated learning.

Parents confess to work pressure, guilt, feeling uncertain of themselves and overwhelmed by their responsibilities. They want their children to get the most out of school but aren't sure how to evaluate what's in place, or how to begin to help.

Teachers ricochet from trying to impart knowledge, to being confidants, social workers, truant officers, nurses, physicians, hygiene and diet advisors, disciplinarians, and bureaucrats.

Today, as children are increasingly exposed to society's negative models and influences, the adults who would otherwise be helping them are in the survivor mode themselves. Consider the following:

Among children, we see an increase in the factors causing negative emotions:

⊖ violence increasing in the media, the neighborhood, or the home, involving children as victims, perpetrators, or fearful witnesses seeking safety

⊖ financial insecurity

⊖ separation and divorce

⊖ absent or busy parents, and feelings of rejection and abandonment

⊖ loneliness and pseudo-sophistication

⊖ an erosion of those experiences and factors which spawn positive emotions

Among both children and adults, we see:

⊖ confusion from redefining the word "family:"

⊖ ⊖ working mothers, single parents, single sex couples, steps and halfs, such products of technology as Donor Dads, Surrogate Moms, and *in vitro* creations, along with some traditional Dick and Jane

Among adults, we see:

⊖ parental fatigue, self-doubt, and confusion:

⊖ ⊖ worry over the amount and nature of time spent together

⊖ ⊖ difficulty budgeting financial and emotional resources

⊖ ⊖ dilution of spontaneous affection

⊖ ⊖ nothing's enough, everything's too much

⊖ teacher burnout as idealism and new realities collide:

⊖ ⊖ class sizes are rising

⊖ ⊖ multi-cultural issues of language and differing cultural behavioral patterns enrich the mix, but add new dimensions of responsibility to the teacher's life and duties

⊖ ⊖ mainstreaming leaves many special needs students in the regular classroom, absorbing teacher time

⊖ ⊖ boundaries between home and school responsibilities blur

⊖ ⊖ budgets decrease, cutting down access to books and eliminating such programs as art, music, sports, library — deemed to be "extras"

⊖ ⊖ supplies of intellectual and psychological energy dwindle at a time of expanding demand

These conditions exist across economic boundaries, and transcend I.Q. scores. They pulse through home and school life. While we acknowledge their urgency, we must resist paralysis, remembering that understanding a situation is the first step to making it better.

Under these circumstances, how can we all work together to help kids learn? We know from common sense, experience, and now neuro-psychological research that positive emotional stances enhance a child's capacity for learning, just as negative ones — some of which become habitual — deplete intellectual energies. First by exploring various emotions, then by addressing their causes and the issues they raise, and finally by suggesting active, positive ways for students to tap into their own capacities, we will see specific ways to keep students' batteries charged.

This is far removed from some current efforts to build self-esteem in 30-minute curriculum modules. Instead, we are addressing the emotions and experiences which nourish self-esteem from within. Strong self-esteem is the flower and fruit of active involvement, emerging competence, exposure to appropriate challenge, and willingness to risk. When we nurture curiosity, creativity, and opportunities for genuine success, self-esteem blooms. Just as denying its role in learning is blindfolding our own eyes, trying to paste it on from the outside is like decorating a child with Post-it Notes.

Enlightened parents understand their role in a child's psychological life. Parental influence spreads far beyond the home, playing a major role in the child's school experience. To help their offspring get the most out of school and life, parents need to weigh the role of emotion in all kinds of learning, and must monitor their own personal, daily, consistent contribution to this aspect of the child's development. This is urgent, considering the beleaguered schools today's children inhabit. *Reach to the heart.*

Enlightened teachers can set the stage for success. By understanding the power of the limbic system — the part of the brain thought to control and direct emotions — to block learning or to liberate thinking, teachers develop an intellectual and scientific foundation for what the good ones already know in their guts: emotionally available children make the most of available opportunities. *Reach to the heart, teach to the head.*

Teachers and parents who work together from a shared set of priorities, such as those in Chapter One, will help one another, as well as themselves, as they help the children in their care.

Emotion: the On/Off Switch for Learning will help the reader:

⊕ understand the influence of the limbic system — the "emotional brain"

⊕ identify classic behaviors and concerns, recognizing psychological or psycho-social stances, and seeing ways of reinforcing the positive and analyzing the negative so as to shift patterns and open new pathways

⊕ develop helpful strategies to use at home and at school, instead of automatically running for outside "counseling"

⊕⊕ recognize the power of parental involvement and dangers of abdication

⊕⊕ recognize the power of teachers: "Good teaching is good therapy" (Anna Freud)

⊕ involve the kid:

⊕⊕ form treaties over such issues as homework

⊕⊕ label the emotion, the behavior, or the event, but not the child

⊕ acknowledge that each of us has probably fit negative categories or felt destructive emotions, and that parents who see their own negative stances in their offspring often feel guilty and angry

⊕ encourage kids to keep risking

⊕ share acceptance that although growth is chaotic,
⊕ ⊕ children who are emotionally available will make the best use of existing support
⊕ ⊕ enlightened adults can clear away much of the debris of negative emotional, behavioral fall-out

This book is designed to help parents and teachers by giving them access to energy and conduits for electricity. Of course, no single strategy, game, or hint will insure a steady pulse of power. Many of the following suggestions are jump-starters: they offer an On button, and a way toward the light.

Priscilla L. Vail
August, 1993
Stonington, Ct.

Chapter ONE

REACHING TO THE HEART, TEACHING TO THE HEAD

Emotion, Learning, and Real Live Kids

B rains are power plants for learning. They work by firing off and receiving electrical impulses. Their interpretive and innovative energies travel along single pathways, vault across spaces, or work through thick bundles of connections.

For power to produce light, heat, or its other miracles, someone or some force has to move the appropriate switch to the On position. If the switch is Off, the power remains only a potential. Nothing happens.

Emotion functions as that switch, either closing or opening pathways to thinking and learning. Parents and teachers who acknowledge a child's predominant emotional stance can reach into and through the feeling, helping the child channel psychological and intellectual energy effectively. Far from imposing additional burdens, this recognition simplifies the job of parenting or teaching, and gives the child a psychological power booster. Often, a combination of common sense and practical suggestions can clear blocked pathways.

This chapter looks first at the location and role of emotion in the human brain. We then explore the interplay of emotion and learning, seeing how and why six guiding principles underlie academic success. The Six Specific Activities for Teachers section of each subsequent chapter relates directly to these guiding principles. Thus, in moving through the book, the reader will see many different ways of bringing these principles to life. Each example is designed to reach to the heart and teach to the head.

If the limbic system — the part of the brain thought to control and direct emotion — is so important, where do we find it and how does it work? To give ourselves general guidelines, we need to look at a triple-axis model of the organization of the child or adult human brain: left/right, back/front, and bottom/top. We will give more space to the latter, since it is central to the points in the book, and because the information is just now becoming generally available.

Left/Right

We can read in heavy tomes or light-weight magazines about the specialized functions of the left and right hemispheres. The left hemisphere is responsible for verbal, linear, sequenced performance, while the right hemisphere is the source of intuitive, global, spatial understanding. It goes without saying that creativity springs from and abides in both domains. Fascinating as it may seem to tease them apart, a more sophisticated view sees how they operate together, since very few children go off to school in the morning leaving one hemisphere sitting at home on the bureau.

The more we learn about the power of interplay between right and left, the more we see the foolishness and danger in oversimplifying a complex process. Recently, I had a phone call from a mother who was in panic from this piece of cockamamie: "Sarah's teacher just told me my child is completely left-brained. What will become of her?"

Back/Front

In considering the second axis, back/front, we can think of the back as the repository for many and varied kinds of information, and the front as the selector, choosing a course of thought or a plan of action. Jane Holmes Bernstein, from Children's Hospital in Boston, used the analogy of the back being like the entire symphony orchestra, and the front being the conductor who tells the musicians whose turn it is to play. The conductor has the whole score, and sees to it that melody, rhythm, and coordination work together to play the piece.

Bottom/Top   Moving from bottom to top, we have what Paul MacLean has called the "Triune Brain." The lowest level, the reptilian brain, contains the *brain stem* — an extension of the spinal cord which houses the arousal system. Next comes the limbic system, the emotional brain, which includes the *hippocampus*, the *amygdala*, and the *hypothalamus*. Above the limbic system is the *cerebral cortex*, which "furnishes us with our most human qualities: our language, our ability to reason, to deal with symbols, and to develop a culture."[1] Because it sits in the middle layer of the bottom/top axis, the limbic system is like a gatekeeper for incoming stimuli, and a dispatcher that sends interpretative messages to higher cortical territories. Here is how the process usually works.

An incoming stimulus first tweaks the arousal system. Arousal sends it up to the limbic system for interpretation, and the limbic system then broadcasts its interpretation of the stimulus up to the cortex.

For example, I may hear the sound of the dishwasher going on, notice it, and understand both the sound and its implications, but it won't rock my emotions one way or another, or unglue my thinking. It will have traveled from arousal to emotion to neocortex, remaining a non-event.

Suppose, however, that my arousal mechanism picks up an unexpected sound. The emotional brain will interpret whether it is something ominous...

perhaps a burglar...or whether it is simply a one-time, unfamiliar, sensory experience. If my limbic system decides the sound is threatening — by itself or by implication — it will broadcast a danger message. In response, the metaphoric pathways, doorways, and windows connecting the limbic system with higher level cortical process will constrict, shrivel, or close down, limiting my access to my own memory, reason, and the ability to make novel connections or to create. Thus, my capacities for thinking and learning are seriously compromised.

If, instead, a positive stimulus reaches my arousal system, arousal pops it on up to the limbic system, and my limbic system says, "Yes! This is entertaining, interesting, of great practical use, sexy, funny, or something I can use to 'astonish family and friends'," the limbic system broadcasts a message of purpose and excitement to the higher neocortex. At that point, the number, the breadth, and the depth of connections between stimulus, emotion, and thinking expand, increasing my access to my own experience and ideas, and enhancing my ability to make novel connections, to reason, and to create. Thus, my capacities for thinking and learning are expanded, extended, and enhanced.

At such moments, the left/right axis, the back/front axis, and the bottom/top axis hum with interconnections, putting the child or adult as actively in touch with his or her capacities as is humanly possible. And, in all humans, the interpretive message from the limbic system — the emotional response to a situation or event — overrides other messages just as a public address system overrides an inter-office phone call.

These interpretations are based on memories of past experiences, as well as immediate reactions to present events. Joseph LeDoux, a psychologist from the Center for Neural Science at New York University, said, "The *hippocampus*, for instance, is involved in recognizing a face and its significance, such as that it's your cousin. The *amygdala* adds that you really don't like him. It offers emotional reactions from memory, independent of your thoughts of the moment about something."[2]

Thus, since past experiences and memories color children's current learning and schooling, wise parents will consciously work to insure that the majority of their children's experiences load them toward a positive limbic response. The general tenor of daily activity before and after school, as well as what happens in class, fosters the emotional response with which the child will meet the world.

Teachers need to recognize their responsibilities to maintain a positive emotional climate in the classroom through their own demeanor, and through the type and variety of methods and materials they use. They also need to be alert to signals of emotional discomfort, understanding and anticipating the probable consequences in the affected child's learning. "Further, we know that coercion and humiliation are poor incentives to serious learning. An affirmed student learns; a hectored student resists. Such is not only warm sentimentality; it is cool efficiency."[3]

To cite a specific example involving math anxiety, a study by Tanis Bryan of the University of Illinois and James Bryan of Northwestern University documents the correlation of positive mood and math performance. "Overall the results of these studies conducted with children find that positive mood improves the amount and rate of learning. Happiness seems to have a positive effect on children's learning, memory, and social behavior. It is believed that positive mood states induce higher levels of activation and faster and more efficient information-processing strategies, whereas sad moods may cause children to become more withdrawn and inattentive."[4]

If all this is so, how is it germane? What kids should we notice and how might we help them? In the classrooms I work in and visit nationwide, I see kids whose academic abilities fit the normal part of the normal curve, but whose intellectual batteries are drained by social/emotional considerations. Irritants to adults and enigmas to themselves, they do not qualify for the increasingly scarce or over-generalized help available to, say, the learning disabled. Yet, their unarticulated difficulties and unmet needs lower the level of group function, and are barriers to personal fulfillment.

Underacknowledged or misunderstood, these students create problems. Recognized and helped, they could release their productive energies. Some are silent sufferers; others are noisy nuisances. A few are dangerous. All are in need. Some of their stories are in this book. Because people's emotional and intellectual development doesn't stop at age 6, fourth grade, or adolescence, several of the case histories in this book follow the child into late childhood or early adulthood.

Concerned adults can help, first by raising their own awareness, next by increasing their own knowledge, and then by taking small, practical, helpful steps. The following section provides a framework.

Six Guiding Principles

Successful child raising and exciting education incorporate six guiding principles. Listing and exploring them will help parents evaluate what their children are receiving both at home and at school, and will help educators assess the academic fare they are offering while also noticing what students bring with them.

These six are found in healthy schools across the nation, be they urban, rural, public, parochial, independent, small, or large — with hefty or marginal budgets. Although any list risks errors of inclusion or exclusion, this collection is built not only on my work and observations, but on long-standing investigations and recommendations by such luminaries as Theodore Sizer, Howard Gardner, Lillian Katz, and James Comer, as well as the experience of several educational/corporate partnerships. These six guiding principles, singly and together, are emotional fuel for learning. They help kids turn the switch to On.

Emotion and intellect fuse through:

1. Prompting Motivation

2. Sparking Curiosity

3. Nourishing Intellect, Talent, and Power

4. Encouraging Connections

5. Assessing Growth

6. Accepting Special Considerations

1. Prompting Motivation

Motivation starts with an idea and a hope, gathers momentum, and sustains a plan. This is the difference between motivation and a passing fancy. People frequently say to me, "Someday I'm going to write a book. Really. I'd like to." What they mean is, "I'd like to *have written* a book, been on Oprah, be rich and famous." Soon, they think of something else and are off on a different pursuit. Motivation and whim differ in length, depth, and intensity.

Under the word *motivation*, my dictionary lists "motive power: the energy, or source of the energy, by which anything is powered." Where do we tap into it? How is it sustained?

Think about a diet. First comes the notion. But, paradoxically, motivation coupled with momentum comes AFTER willpower or exercise melt the first three pounds. The 4-step internal pep talk says:

Others can do it

I'd like to

I can

I did!

Think about learning to play tennis. First, it's an idea. But, the initial act is difficult, humiliating, and sometimes even physically painful. It's tempting to quit. Some people do. Motive power surges AFTER you've hit the sweet spot. You continue trying, hard and often, if you've done it well once. Then,

Others can do it

I'd like to

I can

I did!

The same litany works in school, from Introduction to Trigonometry to learning to decode c-a-t. The first job of teachers and parents is to focus hard on "others can do it," bringing an idea or whim into the realm of possibility. Next, to set the stage so the student really means, "I'd like to," break the task down into manageable chunks and increments. Next, to coach from the sidelines to insure, "I can." Finally, adults need to stand back and get out of the way, letting success belong to the learner who says with wonder, "I DID!"

From diet to sports to academic learning to the murky labyrinths of human psychology, motivation and competence reinforce one another.

Here are some strategies to prompt motivation which we will meet in expanded form later in the book.

⊕ Activate prior knowledge: hitch new information to a familiar concept. It's virtually impossible to join two unknowns.

⊕ Teach kids to ask the five "Plan of Attack" questions:

1. What do I already know?

2. What do I need to find out?

3. Where can I get the information?

4. How will I collect and catalogue it?

5. How will I use it — in what kind of final product?

⊕ insofar as possible, give the "locus of control" to the student: distinctions between "learned helplessness" and "learned optimism," which we will explore on pages 69 and 70, make a critical difference.

⊕ reach different kinds of learners through a variety of approaches, which might include visual aids, manipulatives, and the use of graphs as well as paragraphs. Arrange diverse measures of mastery such as exhibitions, portfolios, or refrigerator displays. Working in the concrete as well the symbolic realm increases the chances of tapping into all students' capabilities.

⊕ find ways to make the new information or technique immediately useful.

⊕ establish goals and standards for mastery/ completion. Reveal them, don't conceal them. Help kids see where they are on THAT path, not in the mark book or some secret "ledger of good people."

⊕ provide opportunities to showcase or display results.

2. Sparking Curiosity

The human may be the only species able to ask a question. This unique capacity opens a door to understanding which must be both guarded and opened, if real learning is to occur. My friend and mentor, a Professor of Child Development at Bank Street College of Education, says that when she was a little girl returning home from school, her father, a rabbi, would be waiting at the door to scoop her up, give her a kiss, and say "Leah, what good questions did you ask today?"

We need to revere the messiness of questions as well as the tidiness of answers. Children who have been trained that the main goal of schooling is to give correct answers are limited to learning from other people's discoveries.

True learning, at home or at school, is highly aggressive. True reading, although done sitting down, is active — not passive.

What should we do? To spark curiosity, let's first find out what our children are interested in learning about. If they are interested in clothing and food of other cultures, or games children played in different times, or what happens to animals when they hibernate, we can frequently tailor our classroom investigations — as well as individual projects and family conversations — to match the interest. Sometimes, we have to be sneaky and bait the trap, by linking what we know students are already interested in to what we believe it is important for them to learn.

⊕ teachers and parents who honor originality over conformity make curiosity and risk-taking safe. The error half of trial and error is the source of some glorious mistakes and original discoveries.

⊕ the tenets of cooperative learning — in which problems are tackled by small working groups, instead of unwieldy whole classes or solitary moles — are suitable for home as well as school. They open avenues for curiosity.

⊕ to sustain curiosity, give the learner some latitude and choice in how to demonstrate new capacities or knowledge. Being shackled to mandatory, three-page, topic-sentence book reports is a quick way to send a budding reader off to Nintendo.

⊕ adults should double-check kids' understanding of the concepts of space and of time, as well as their receptive and expressive language levels, in order to be sure the children have the conceptual foundations needed to knit the familiar and the unfamiliar together. There is no point in trying to spark curiosity about *aborigines* of the *archipelago* among children who have neither knowledge of geography nor the concept of first settlers. Think back to Motivation, and breaking tasks down into manageable chunks.

3. Nourishing Intellect, Talent, and Power

To establish this principle and the learning it prompts, we need to promote three good R's and prohibit one bad one. Desirables are: *Receive, Ruminate,* and *Respond.* The miscreant is *Regurgitate.*

Receive is easy. Adults in the child's life want him or her to receive accurate factual information, aesthetically appealing experiences, and opportunities which nourish imagination. In addition, some aspects of *Receive* involve rote learning, a threshold to be crossed in entering a new discipline.

Through *Rumination,* the learner absorbs what is offered, mulls it over, makes connections to memory and the intellectual or emotional storehouse, and soaks the new information in existing connotations, so it becomes a central part of the person's thinking and feeling. This takes time and privacy.

Neurologists are now exploring the concept of *convergent zones*, interconnections of thought which give many dimensions to a single word or object.[4] For example, the word *cup* may call to mind the function of a cup, or the physical properties of a cup, or the type of cup the listener or reader owns or aspires to own, or the shape of the word in print, or the strings of sound necessary to speak or spell cup, or words which rhyme with cup. The list is endless. Of course, the greater the number of associations, the richer the web of convergent zones, and the greater the variety and texture of thought available to the thinker.

"Our memories are stitching and knitting all the time the fabulous tapestry of our associative inner lives such that we are, in our present lives, always connected through memory to the vastness of our pasts, in all the details and arresting vividness of the original events."[5]

How do we support this part of the learning process? The richer the child's experience and exposure to ideas, the more creatively complex his or her convergent zones will be.

After *Receive* and *Ruminate*, the stage is set for *Respond*. By this I mean the opportunity to make a creative product through words (written or spoken), or the arts, or a model expressing the learner's reactions to what has been learned. The child who reads or hears a story might make a diorama showing major scenes from the narrative, or a set of drawings, or one drawing showing a favorite episode, or might pantomime part of the story, or design a set and costumes for a dramatization, or write a book report, or talk to a friend, or act out being one of the characters. This is a far cry from the stultifying *Regurgitate*.

Occasionally, one still sees teachers or parents who read a story (or ask the children to read it), and then ask such questions as "What color was the girl's dress?", "How many children were in the family and what were their names?", "Where were they going in the car?" Retrieving and regurgitating factual information represents one kind of mental process, but not one which I would call thinking. *Why* and *how* are questions which tap into the depth and breadth of receiving and ruminating.

Sometimes, teachers or parents will say, "There isn't time for *Ruminate*. There's too much to cover." In my experience, it is far better to read three books and exercise the three good R's than to read six books, leapfrogging from *Receive* to *Respond*. A wise friend once said to me, "The purpose of studying a subject is not to cover it, but to uncover it."

If we skip right over from *Receive* to *Respond*, we steal the child's chance to make the information, concept, or story part of a personal intellectual/emotional matrix through *Rumination*. How does this work across different disciplines?

Rumination belongs to mathematics as much as it does to language arts or science. *Regurgitation* is the companion of arithmetic.

Wrongly, because some adults overlook the distinction between arithmetic and mathematics, many children think the terms are synonymous. Pencil-paper arithmetic demands tidy numeral formation, straight columns, and accurate (often rapid) computation. Correct answers are the keys to the kingdom.

Mathematics is the realm of questions. It is both a language and a symbol system through which the learner can explore the ordering principles of our universe. Yet, some young thinkers with sophisticated mathematical ideas are weak in arithmetical tallying and recording. As we have mentioned before and will see again, strength in the 3-Dimensional realm (mathematics, science, engineering, the arts, hands-on learning, and knowing how to fix broken machinery) often coexists with weakness in the 2-Dimensional symbolic realms of reading, writing, spelling, handwriting, and pencil-paper arithmetic. When this happens, young students — male or female — may mistakenly decide they are "lousy in math," when in fact they are weak in numeral writing and memorized calculation. The world turns off natural mathematicians through this misinterpretation.

We need to include playfulness, novelty, and exploration in math. Experiences outside of school, such as surfing the supermarket, are ideal for estimating, tallying, and seeing different results from different ways of spending twenty bucks. In school or at home, playing with patterns and solving puzzles with tangrams or geoboards bring excitement to the fore and mastery within reach. Asking kids to see how many ways they can find to build a number demonstrates the alternatives which are part of the fascination of math. Just last week, a first grade class was building the number 20. Some of their ideas were: 10 + 10, 30 - 10, 10 + 2 + 8, 20 x 1, 20 - 0, and 5 x 3 + 5.

Many teachers or parents, non-scientists themselves, avoid this discipline because they are afraid they don't know enough. Sadly, particularly in middle schools, science instruction emphasizes regurgitation: read a section, memorize lists, take a written test. True science, in contrast, invites the learner to 1) make a hypothesis, 2) observe, 3) decide whether empirical observations confirm or contradict the idea, 4) figure out why, and 5) map new ways to get similar results in parallel experiments, or 6) devise novel applications for the knowledge.

"I wonder...", "Maybe...", "Do you suppose...", and "Let's try..." are the *lingua franca* of the scientist. These are the same questions which enlist intellect, talent, and power. Science is for questioners. "If they had wanted to stay safe, Galileo would have trained his telescope on the building next door, and Darwin would have stuck to pigeons."[6]

In the arts, we want to expose children to excellent models, introduce them to classical techniques, but then encourage them to break out on their own, avoiding the "How to Copy a Flower" concept — another form of regurgitation: ®

To nourish intellect, talent and power we need to:

⊕ discard the notions that we can spot intelligence primarily by hunting for high test scores, and that it belongs exclusively to pale, owl-eyed students who lurk in the library. We need to expand our own perceptions and definitions to include the traits of intelligence, power, and talent delineated by Galaburda, Gardner, Kaufman, Renzulli, Sternberg, and Vail, which we will explore in considerable detail in the last chapter. (Also see the Resource Section for specific titles.)

⊕ decide what aspect of intellect, talent, or power we're really trying to reach, and then aim specifically for that area, instead of running around aimlessly with an academic cattle prod.

⊕ find, meet, and acknowledge what Howard Gardner refers to as the 5-year-old thinker inside each of us. In *The Unschooled Mind, How Children Think and How Schools Should Teach Them*, Gardner points to countless examples of students who have learned formulaic operations in class, but do not use these precepts in thinking about the real world. Even smart kids with diplomas from fancy institutions are vulnerable to this kind of laminated learning — glued on from the outside but not interwoven with the child's intellectual matrix. To do justice to intellect, we must lead the thinker, instead, to what Gardner calls Christopherian Encounters (named for Christopher Columbus) — a kind of thinking in which intellect and reason override the obvious truth that the world is flat.

⊕ remember that children who are gifted in the 3-D world (math, science, engineering, the arts, athletics, etc.) may be at risk for 2-D endeavors with printed symbols (letters, words, numerals, process signs in arithmetic). Although detailed solutions do not belong in this section, this seems the right place to underscore that these children need multi-sensory teaching, access to the concrete as well as the abstract, and chances to explain, display, and demonstrate what they have learned. Harking back to Motivation, intellectual appetite is whetted by success.

⊕ provide opportunities for kids to be smart without being embarrassed.

⊕ avoid the rush to the *appearance* of knowledge: surface, speedy, temporary.

⊕ avoid the dilemma of the prisoners of perfection — children whose identities are so linked to getting the highest grades or having their perfect papers displayed on the walls of the school or refrigerator, they're afraid to risk a novel thought:

⊖ ⊖ the junior scholastic Faust who sells eagerness to question for a set of correct answers

⊖ ⊖ the pint-size cynic who cons the system so successfully that true hard work no longer offers merit or excitement

⊖ ⊖ the Tidy Little Girl whose unbitten pencils write correct answers in blanks in workbooks from the supermarket, who memorizes and recites easily, who convinces others (and herself) that she is gifted when in fact she is merely meticulous.

4. Encouraging Connections Children who make connections move eagerly from one subject to another, shifting from the vocabulary and concepts of math to those of language arts or social studies, adjusting their frames of reference when it's time to change classes. At the same time, they see how and why what they learned in social studies is useful in creative writing, or how the arithmetic they are learning in school parallels setting a budget or tallying baseball averages. One might say their convergent zones converge on one another.

Eagerness to make connections is one of the hallmarks of intelligent thinking. It depends on being able to make distinctions, and on orderly *filing*, smooth *retrieval*, and ease in *recombining*.

Filing

The efficient learner, who will make connections easily, mentally files emotional, physical, and intellectual experiences in an orderly way. Language is the foundation and the tool.

Being disorganized is quicksand to efficient learning. Yet, many intelligent children have littered or misplaced mental files, thus their retrieval systems — which may have been grope and grab operations to begin with — are compromised. Not surprisingly, their efforts at recombining enjoy irregular, sporadic success. These difficulties are aggravated by (and often caused by) problems with language.

Categories for efficient filing include the six *wh* words (*who, what, when, where, why, how*). Who was involved — one or many? What was the main event? When did it occur? Where did it take place? Why does it matter? How does it relate to other experiences or perceptions?

Retrieving

Smooth memory function allows a thinker to select needed information from the vast convergent zones of personal experience, emotion, and thought. And, of course, effortless retrieval depends on orderly filing. Otherwise, retrieval is like rummaging around in the socks drawer at night with no lights on.

Disruptions of retrieval are embarrassing, annoying, or disastrous. Some people have trouble with rote memory. Even though they have wide and accurate memory for experiences and feelings, they have trouble memorizing arithmetic combinations, lists of presidents or monarchs in succession, or scientific formulae.

Others may have trouble with target word retrieval. They know exactly what they want to say but the necessary word is "just on the tip of my tongue." Stymied by retrieval, these clutterers fill their speech with time buyers such as *and um, the um, like, you know*, and indefinite markers and pronouns in place of names. They describe objects by function instead of label.

At Show and Tell, Marcia said, "We went, you know...me and my family...to that place where they have the um...um...it's blue and like tall, and sloshy, but I forgot to bring mine cuz I wasn't sure we were really going to go, at least, well, not then, maybe. So, and my cousin, which is fatter than I am, had two but I didn't want to, you know, sort of have my brother make fun of me, so instead I...Well, Mom says we can go another time."

The other children, not to mention the teacher, were totally confused. Also bored. One said, "Hey Marcia, why don't you draw it on the board?" After two or three expertly drawn lines, the kids said in unison, "Oh. The water slide!"

Marcia had been trying to say, "My family and I went to the water slide. I forgot to take my bathing suit because I wasn't sure we were really going there. My cousin Julie, who is fatter than I am, had two bathing suits, but I didn't want to wear one because I was afraid my brother would laugh at me, so I just watched, but Mom says we can go back another time."

Recombining

Originality and creativity are expressed through novel combinations of ideas, concepts, or experiences. The thinker-learner files, retrieves, and then recombines. Doing this with efficiency, as well as enthusiasm, requires a rich supply of raw material, systematic filing as a foundation for precision in retrieval, and finally, the new and personal idea.

Those who are intrigued by this will find further amplification in *Learning Styles* (see the Resource Section), as well as in the earlier section, Nourishing Intellect, Talent, and Power.

Four great writers and thinkers express the importance of the above.

⊕ on the importance of a wide and firm factual foundation, Pasteur wrote "Chance favors the prepared mind."

⊕ on the need for interweavings, E.M. Forster wrote in *Howards End* "Only connect!"

⊕ on the need for releasing imagination, Einstein wrote "My gift for fantasy has meant more to me than my capacity to acquire positive information."

⊕ on the need for ethical vision beyond the immediate excitement of discovery, Professor Abraham Tannenbaum of Columbia University spoke of the need to recognize "the moral consequences of having a very good idea."

5. Assessing Growth

While tests and testing are a fact of life, educators have progressed beyond thinking that the only way for a student to show learning is to write for three hours (or 45 minutes) in a test book in a proctored study hall. Some students perform exceedingly well under such circumstances. They are fortunate. Other students, who may know the material well and may have participated eagerly and constructively in class discussions, freeze. For both the fortunate and the unfortunate, the teacher in such situations plays the role of captor — possessor of the finite number of correct answers, a roster against which the students' efforts will be tallied. The underlying sense is that the teacher is out to catch the student in varying degrees of "un-knowledge," and "take off points" accordingly.

Now, moving far beyond this grim scenario, we have such concepts as performance-based assessment, exhibitions, and portfolios. Why and how do these work? Are these some new-fangled mollycoddlings from lazy-minded flower children? No. These procedures, in place in some of the nation's most academically rigorous schools, recognize that children — like the rest of us — enjoy demonstrating new competencies. They like to strut their stuff. These ways of measuring mastery encourage and display the habits of mind Theodore Sizer lays out for us: perspective, analysis, imagination, empathy, communication, commitment, humility, joy. In other words, emotional engagement and intellectual growth.

By expanding the avenues for students to demonstrate mastery, we remove destructive anxiety and accommodate constructive energy. We Reach to the Heart as we Teach to the Head. The teacher shifts from captor to coach, from adversary to ally. These practices create a positive emotional climate while maintaining or raising academic standards. And guess what disappears? Cheating.

Here are some examples.

⊕ exhibitions can include such wide ranging manifestations as dioramas, skits, mock newspapers, models, works of fiction, or dance performances. One fourth grade class had been studying early settlements in the United States. They turned their classroom into a museum. Each small group was responsible for developing an exhibit showing life in one of the settlements. They were to make, draw, design, and show as many facets of life in this settlement as possible, and be prepared to describe how it differed from others. Each student in the class was responsible for being a docent for one part of the museum, BUT, since they didn't know which area, they had to be prepared for all of them. Finally, they were assigned their stations, given a few days to polish their information, and then for two days other classes came to visit the Museum of Early Settlement.

In another instance, a group had been studying Athens in the 5th century B.C. Rather than give them a test, the teacher asked the class to brainstorm what topics a comprehensive newspaper about the era would cover. The group decided on local, national, and international news, editorial opinion, political happenings, gossip, sports, drama and entertainment, finance, war, education, births, marriages, obituaries, book reviews, and...comics!

The teacher broke the class into small groups, each being responsible for one topic. The class elected a senior editor, layout and production staff, and they were off. It goes without saying that all students in that class had to be knowledgeable about the period in order to have enough substantiated information. The pride in the final product told the real tale. Jeb, a student who had never enjoyed school and never invested himself in any academic area, said, "It's great to show what you know!"

The science teacher who lets students choose between making a model of a concept or writing an essay about it is honoring different learning styles, allowing for joy, and demonstrating faith that the kids know what they have learned.

"The exhibition then is not only the target. It is also a representation of the way one prepares to reach the target. That is, school is about practicing to wrap one's mind around real and complex ideas, those of fundamental consequences for oneself and for the culture. It is not merely about 'coverage,' or being informed, or displaying skills. It is the demonstration of the employment of all of these toward important and legitimate ends."[7]

⊕ portfolios show the evolution of competence. While some schools are using them incorrectly as models of perfected performance, the original design — which expresses the philosophical intention — shows pieces of work from the beginning of a process or competence, gives indications of problems to be addressed and suggestions offered, then shows work from the next stage with teacher and student comments, and then a work of the moment. The portfolio can be made of drawings, essays, poetry, fiction, photographs, or videotapes of art projects. Portfolio assessment is designed to show growth in an area, sustained interest, habits of perseverance, and the absorption of new learning. It is NOT designed to be a petal-plucking good/bad, perfect/imperfect exercise. To focus on the perfection of the end product is to miss the point completely.

⊕ Arts Propel is a project, begun by Howard Gardner and Educational Testing Service in the Pittsburgh public schools, designed to assess work in the arts. Combining portfolio development with teacher training in evaluation, the project — now in its fifth year — is designed to open the field of testing to young people who want to show their prowess.

⊕ a few of the many additional measures of mastery which allow kids to show what they know without tears or panic:

   ⊕ ⊕ open-book tests

   ⊕ ⊕ take-home tests

   ⊕ ⊕ test answers spoken into a classroom tape recorder

The parent whose child's school already incorporates these practices owes those teachers a vote of confidence, and a personal thank you. Parents whose children's schools are not there yet might show this section to the appropriate administrator and volunteer to procure pertinent books from the Resource Section through the public library system, if the school does not already have them. The parent whose kids are stuck in a rigidly traditional system can incorporate some of these ideas for home projects. The point is to whet kids' appetites for new knowledge and competence by providing opportunity, learning...AND a showcase.

6. Accepting Special Considerations

This book is not specifically about atypical learners: the gifted and talented, those who struggle with the various dyslexias, those burdened by intellectually or physically handicapping conditions, those who speak little or no English yet may be fluent in another tongue, those ensnared by the hydra of poverty. Each of these groups has advocates. Fine books have been written on their behalf. The Resource Section may help both parents and teachers find reliable information, descriptive anecdotal material, and clinical strategies.

However, many of the children represented in this book are also dyslexic, or learning disabled, or gifted and talented, or inadequately fed, housed, and loved. Children overflow categories, and their needs and postures overlap. While these children may need special support, extra teaching, or tutoring, the exercises and strategies in this book will still be helpful.

Each of the ensuing chapters deals with an emotional stance or social/emotional circumstance, discussing likely causes and probable results. Each chapter then includes a section titled Ten Tips For Moms, Dads, Nannies, Grannies, Grandfathers, Teachers, and Other Concerned Adults; another section titled Six Specific Activities for Teachers; and a concluding section called One Child's Story.

Because all people experience a wide range of emotions, parents of a confident child will still profit from reading the chapter about anger, or the one about structure. Who knows what next week — or next year's teacher — may bring? Understanding what goes on inside many children helps in understanding one or a few, and vice versa.

Parents will also benefit from reading the sections for teachers, as a way of understanding why some methods and materials may be used in classrooms, and as a way of having in reserve some steps to take at home if school offerings are disappointing or destructive. The ideal situation is for parents and teachers to meet, confer, and understand and respect one another, so they can cooperate on behalf of the children they share.

Of course, no single exercise, no individual game, no solitary sentence can alter deep feelings. The suggestions and exercises to come are offered as launchpads, beginnings, and representative examples of what has worked in literally thousands of households and classrooms.

Each of us can taste success. Since confidence is a goal for all children, let's begin there.

Chapter TWO

CHILDREN AND CONFIDENCE

Joyful Purpose, Purposely Joyful

The parent or teacher of an already confident child can learn — from the examples and words of children themselves — how to maintain momentum. Similarly, we need to explore ways to instill and foster confidence in a child who is timid or pessimistic. Why do we need to bother? The combination of joyful emotional energy and purposeful, successful learning is both unmistakable and unbeatable. As we will see in this chapter, confident children — by their nature and outlook — are self-fulfilling prophesies.

Whether extroverted or serious and dignified, confident children mine their own assets. Sometimes socially boisterous, sometimes emotionally high-spirited, sometimes studiously successful, sometimes quietly purposeful, confident people — comfortable with themselves — have much to teach us all.

Both actually and metaphorically, confident children expand, contract, flex, dip, lunge, sway, leap, vault, press, respond, bounce back, mobilize, and regroup as they rally their ideas, emotions, past experiences, current plans, and future expectations in a choreography of optimism.

Confidence is the fruit of competence. The old adage holds true: nothing succeeds like success. And, success appears in many ways and among many different kinds of children. We find confident children in the top, middle, and even low group of every class in school, and — in family life — they are sprinkled across birth order and gender.

To recognize true confidence when we meet it, and to see when, where, and how it flowers, we need to ask two sets of questions:

Set One

a) **Are these children selectively blessed? Are they winners in some lottery of entitlement?**

b) **Can confidence be fostered?**

c) **Can confidence be restored once bruised?**

d) **Can confidence be extinguished?**

The single answer to these multiple questions is "Yes."

Set Two

a) **Does confidence only coexist with giftedness or extremely high IQ?**

b) **Must kids who struggle in school lose their confidence?**

c) **Are learning disabled kids automatically exiled from confidence?**

d) **Does confidence make people stuck-up?**

The single answer to these multiple questions is "No."

Let's explore Set One.

a) **Are these children selectively blessed? Are they winners in some lottery of entitlement?**

Each child has a flair, an interest, a direction, which magnetizes the child's internal compass needle to a personal North, and which can be a source of genuine confidence. This interest may be determined:

genetically

environmentally

randomly, temporarily, cumulatively mysteriously

Many talents and untalents pass down through heredity, directly from one generation to another or skipping. The example which pops to my mind involves posture, a grandfather, a small boy, and the graceful, athletic prowess which feeds legitimate, unboastful pride.

Although the grandfather is not a military school graduate, his bearing is noticeable for the straightness of his spine, the way he carries his head, and the rhythmic roll of his walk. He is also — chicken or egg — a remarkably graceful skater and dancer. Seeing him walk down the street with his grandson, the watcher wants to say, "Honey, I shrunk the grandfather." The same distinctive head carriage, the same rolling gait, the same straight spine. The grandson started skating early because everyone sensed he would be a natural. At age 6, he already has two years of ice experience. This year, he will start playing hockey. He moves as if born to blades. He stands tall partly because of an inherited trait, and partly because he knows he uses his body with grace and power.

Some interests bloom because the environment is ideal. I think of the example of two young families. The mothers are sisters; one husband is a teacher, a cartoonist, a coach, and a renaissance man with a glorious sense of play. The other husband is an artist — a master builder with an exciting, innovative architectural eye and keen aesthetic sense. Together, these families, who live 300 miles apart, have five children close of an age — two girls and three boys. When they get together, there is never a problem of how to amuse the children. There is always a generous supply of paper, pencils, markers, or crayons. By the hour, these five make books, write stories, design catalogues, create menus, invent animals, or write a family newspaper. Of course, heredity must play a part, but so does environment. Both homes are filled with paper, scissors, colors, glue, and other raw materials, and, happily, all five children gravitate in their direction. These children, singly and together, deeply enjoy their artistic talents and delight in sharing their creations. Confidence flourishes as they see the enjoyment their unpressured, spontaneous efforts bring.

Some interests bloom randomly, temporarily, or cumulatively. A young woman who today is a mother, an award-winning quilter, a computer whiz, and a film editor was variously fascinated in her childhood by dogs, cats, and horses, skiing, machine sewing, hand embroidery, math, drama, ballet, and playing the trumpet. Her preadolescence was a potpourri of lessons. Partly because of changing interests, partly because of acceleration, partly because of geography, she attended six schools and colleges in the six years between tenth grade and earning her B.A. She wasn't flighty as much as she was voracious. The result is that, today, she knows how to do a lot of things, and tackles new learning with optimism born of past successes.

Some interests bloom mysteriously from an alchemy whose recipe is hidden, but whose results are unmistakable, as in the case of a young man named Peter Boal. The second child and only son of a trial lawyer and his social worker wife, Peter lived in the suburbs and went to a local school, where he was an excellent student and a fine athlete. One Christmas, when he was 7, his parents took him to see the *Nutcracker Suite* at Lincoln Center in New York. He was mesmerized, remembered everything he had seen, and persuaded his parents to take him a second and third time. When he read in the program that there was a school attached to the company, he begged to be allowed to go, promising to keep up with his regular studies at his school in the country, if he could be allowed to do this, too. His parents made the arrangements, and, partly because he is private by nature and partly to avoid teasing, Peter told no one.

One day he came home from ballet distressed, saying he couldn't seem to memorize the steps and routines. He wondered if he should move from the front row to a back row where he could watch and follow other dancers. Not knowing where their certainty came from, his parents told him to stay right where he was, to dance what was inside of him.

The rest is an exciting history. Rising steadily through the ranks, continuing to receive accolades as the pyramid thinned at the top, he has become a principal dancer for the company. George Balanchine said of him as a little boy, "This is the kind of talent that comes along once in a century. But, I can't guarantee he'll be able to keep it through and after adolescence."

He did, and is newly married to another dancer. Who knows whether their children will be as graceful as their parents, or average walkers like their four grandparents. There have been no dancers or outstanding athletes on either side of either family as far back as anyone can remember.

The adult's job is to spot proclivities and provide opportunities for growth. Parents must notice and nurture, sharing their perceptions of their child with the school. Teachers must identify and intensify — spotting, highlighting, and exercising the specific interests and capabilities which surface during the school day. Together, teachers and parents who offer both praise and practice will help confidence bloom.

b) Can confidence be fostered?

Fostered, yes. Injected, no. Nor will confidence grow in a vacuum. Its development requires:

interest

opportunity

exercise

recognition

The flowering of confidence depends also on "explanatory style."[1] The person who says, "I had good luck" is dependent on fate. The person who says, "I made that happen" feels effective. Erik Erikson tells us that school-age children and people of all ages absorb this judgement: "I am what I can make work."

To help children feel confident, we are wise to depend on them instead of simply praising them. Again, "nothing succeeds like success." Find a talent, skill, or interest, discuss and recognize it with the child, create a need for it, and weave that need and talent into the fabric of daily living. Practice and exercise the ability. Keep it going. Find ways to extend the ability into new fields. Utopia? Takes too much time? Meet Jeff.

Jeff was what I would call a "meat and potatoes" boy. Not too imaginative, fond of order, comfortable in routines, he has always liked numbers. He will probably be a contented, reliable accountant as an adult. As a young child and during his early school years, he was physically timid, and — although he learned to throw and catch a ball — he feared and disliked contact sports. This particular reluctance takes a tremendous toll on a school-age boy. It's virtually impossible for kids who avoid such games as soccer and football to earn a spot in the "in" group.

His parents relied on Jeff's organization and reliability. If he helped pack the picnic hamper, there would always be the right number of forks, and he wouldn't forget the cups. He could be counted on to collect the correct number of hot dogs or desserts or boxes of juice at the supermarket. He organized the goody bags for his siblings' birthday parties, and even made his own after the disastrous year when other people did them and came out with one too few on the big day.

When Jeff hit second grade, he discovered graphing. He graphed the birthdays in his class by month, the numbers of missing teeth, the number of chocolate chips in three different brands of chocolate chip cookies, and the wins, ties, and losses of the teams in the local soccer and baseball leagues. He became the resident statistician — a highly regarded fellow, keeper of records — and because children (and people of all ages) confer power on whatever is written down, in a superstitious way Jeff became a custodian of victory, thus a good man to know and a valuable friend.

In his teens, he kept statistics for sports and for rock groups — their members, their hit songs, their road tours, and their recordings. When it was time for the class play, he let others do the imagining, the memorizing, the proclaiming. He managed the props. Jeff doesn't like athletics and contact sports any more than he did as a young child, but he, his parents, and his teachers have found ways for him to be important and feel proud.

He knows what he's good at. Others value what he does. Confidence!

c) Can confidence be restored once bruised?

The answer is yes, but the task requires effort on two fronts:

1. re-value the overlooked competence

2. re-value the person who possesses that competence

Russel Hoban wrote a book for children of all ages, *How Tom Fooled Captain Najork and His Hired Sportsmen*. In the story, a hapless but clever boy named Tom is in the clutches of his guardian, Aunt Fidget Wonkham-Strong, who wears an iron hat and forces him to eat "greasy bloaters and mutton sog," and to memorize multiple pages of the Nautical Almanac. Tom would rather fool around.

To teach him the worthlessness of his fooling around, Aunt Fidget Wonkham-Strong sends for Captain Najork and his hired sportsmen, to challenge Tom in games of Muck, Sneedball, and Womble.

Three cheers for re-valuing the competence. All that fooling around has given Tom the skills he needs for a handy victory. He foists Aunt Fidget off on poor Capt. Najork, and via the yellow pages, gets himself a new guardian, Aunt BundleJoy CosySweet, who wears a flowered hat and believes boys need lots of fooling around time. Three cheers for re-valuing the person who possesses that competence! Yay, Tom.

A similar story in a more serious vein involves Stephen, a dreamy, pudgy boy, the only child born to a pair of outdoorsy, no-nonsense, concrete thinkers. As a child, Stephen gravitated to arts and crafts and to fantasy. Highly imaginative, with a powerful visual/tactile sense, he made puppets, puppet shows, stage sets, and he dressed up in costumes. His parents tried to cajole or coerce him into other behaviors. Outwardly polite and seemingly cooperative, he played out of their sight as much as possible, and hid his creations from them.

At adolescence, these interests and proclivities remained. He was extremely active in the backstage aspects of the school theater department. He became skillful with lighting, set design, and remarkably creative in costuming. His parents were terrified.

At one performance, a Broadway professional, who was in the audience watching another child, saw Stephen's work and praised it to the skies. Only then did his parents see value. External confirmation from a famous person gave them the courage to look at what their son could do. Sad but true, they still didn't understand the mysteries and magic of his work, but they could acknowledge it to be praiseworthy. The continuing encouragement of the well-known adult, who is Stephen's mentor now, has launched him well on the way to a successful career.

Teachers in school can find among their colleagues the professionals who can assess and praise what a student is producing. Kids often don't know how to value what they do easily, particularly if other academic work is difficult. I heard one say, "If it's easy, it doesn't count." Just as teachers may not value ideas and paths of thinking which lead away from the prescribed curriculum, parents may not value their offspring's output if it is in a field apart from what they know.

Therefore, we need to remember to permit individual interest, provide opportunity for exercise, and find recognition, as we re-value the competence in order to restore confidence.

d) Can confidence be extinguished?

The learning child sends out feelers of exploration, sometimes shyly, sometimes unselfconsciously, sometimes recklessly. In addition to seeking, these are also the child's offerings of generosity: smiles, words, footsteps, ideas, insights, feelings. If they constantly meet rebuke or ridicule, they will shrivel, shatter, wither, drop away, or their energies will be driven underground.

As we see in the examples of the histories of countries in Central and Eastern Europe, it is possible to paralyze initiative by punishing originality and ambition while rewarding obedience, particularly when the people are kept in suspense about the supply of food and shelter, and have been subdued into dependence on the state. There is a parallel to school.

If the teacher in control values only compliance and reluctantly doles out the few high grades sufficient to make the honor roll, the results will be either toadying students or turned off kids. We can extinguish confidence in school by creating suspense over grading, and by marking off points for originality. In such situations, when the "locus of control" belongs solely to the teacher, the twin companions of competence and confidence do not grow. Kids feel like beggars, not creators.

Tenth grade Rebecca, writing a science exam and unable to remember the words "migrating flock," referred to "a flying wedge." The answer was marked wrong in red pen. The comment read, "This course is science, not poetry."

At home or at school, adults can extinguish confidence by inadvertently doing any one of the following, which are hurtful individually and lethal in combination.

finding fault vs. finding a good job

"You've left off the forks!" vs. "You've got the spoons, glasses, and napkins. Good start. What do you need to finish?"

doing FOR rather than WITH

"Here. I'll do it. We don't have all day." vs. "Good job with the snow pants and boots. I'll help with the zipper, if you want me to."

sending messages of expected failure

"No wonder it burned. You can't have read the recipe — there isn't any liquid. Move over. I'll fix it." vs. "Let's try that recipe again tomorrow. We'll get it. Let's try lining up all the ingredients before we start to cook."

giving too hard a job

Remember our discussion of four steps of motivation on pages 7 and 8. The first job of adults is to make the task possible by breaking it down into manageable increments. Instead of saying, "Figure out how long it will take you to...", say, "This job has x parts to it. Let's see how much time each will take, add them together, and throw in a little extra in case of emergency." This leads to success, rather than "Can't you ever finish anything?"

requiring repetition of a boring job

Sometimes, competent children are required to keep on doing (Practicing?!) something they've already shown they have mastered. I heard a teacher last week say to Wendy, "You're so good at these long division problems, I've given you two extra sheets of them."

changing the ground rules midway through a project

"OK. You're half way there. Now, instead of finishing with biographical sketches of three major figures, why don't you do what the other class is doing. They're...I think they're...working up a time line of all the events we've been talking about. Well, actually you can do the bios, OR the time line. As a matter of fact, you can do both if you want, or if you have some better idea, let me know."

using sarcasm or humiliation

The precept is this: NEVER use sarcasm with children. NEVER use humiliation to enforce discipline. My mind is still seared by the memory of a school assembly with some parents and community members in attendance. The teacher in charge singled out one member of the student body and called him by name saying, "And, I'm talking to you, John Smith. I told you if you talked during this assembly I would humiliate you publicly. You did, and here is that public humiliation as promised."

This is the place for two additional comments. First, during adolescence confidence is under daily attack from inner foes. It is as though kids' blood vessels are filled with hungry hormones racing through the tubes like Pac-Man, devouring confidence wherever it lurks. How impossible it would be to feel confident about such things as school work or friendships or athletic ability or talent or ideas, if you went to sleep each night not knowing how big your nose would be in the morning, where your arms would end, or where you might grow a zit.

Consequently, a young person may either go into intellectual hiding for fear of ridicule, or may take on boisterous bluster to cover up insecurity. Treated appropriately, these children will regain their equilibrium. While they are in flux, however, they need many of the underlying supports, strategies, and techniques which are helpful to younger children, and which are found in later sections of this chapter.

Second, there are some children who overcome seemingly impossible odds. They have resilience. Where does this come from? What are some steps to bolster resilience? In *Overcoming the Odds: High Risk Children from Birth to Adulthood*, the authors mention five factors:

⊕ Everyone had at least one person who unconditionally accepted them as they were.

⊕ One teacher who takes a personal interest in the child — or acts as a role model, counselor, or confidante — can be a powerful force for resilience.

⊕ An at-risk child who shows a particular talent or proclivity feels legitimate pride and comes across as a winner to the others.

⊕ Children who have an instinctive optimism that things will work out are more resilient than their pessimistic peers. This is not prompted by circumstantial reality: some see the glass as half full, others see it half empty.

⊕ Children who care for others (people or pets) develop a sense of responsibility which nourishes resilience.

In forthcoming chapters, we will explore Howard Gardner's work on "multiple intelligences," discuss the importance of being givers as well as receivers, and consider the special potential of mentor relationships in young people's lives. We can BE those forces for children, as well as read about them.

Writing about the late New Yorker Magazine editor, William Shawn, Roger Angell said it this way: "It's something a child would do, and children can never get enough praise, particularly if it comes in the form and person of an adult who will give them full attention: attention beyond measure. Praise makes them grow and go on, and those who bestow it are remembered vividly, even after they are gone."[2]

Moving to the second set of questions, let's meet some real live children and listen to their own words.

a) Does confidence only coexist with giftedness or extremely high IQ?

Secure in her place among the top group, called "Bluebirds," in first grade, Penelope wrote with a strong hand, read with conviction, and laughed with enjoyment. A story she wrote that year said: *"I am a princess. My name is Becky. I live in a castle. Every day I go in the garden. I pick flowers. I like my home. I go in all the passageways. I sleep in a royal bed. I wear royal clothes. When I go outside I go over the drawbridge. I love being a princess. The End."*

Perhaps it is worth noting that Penelope lives with her siblings, parents, and grandmother in a very small apartment in a neighborhood sociologists would call "socio-economically deprived." News reporters call it a "hot spot." Residents call it "the Towers." Her glistening imagination comes from her powerful, internal, intellectual forces, not from her environment.

b) Must kids who struggle in school lose their confidence?

In the same grade, but a lower academic echelon, Brian was a "Cardinal." His academic successes were won with the sweat of his brow, and he frequently interrupted his writing to shake his hand and look at his fingers, as if to ask why they didn't print more smoothly. Here's the story he wrote: *"Hi! My name is King John. I am a king. I own a stone castle. And I am in my dining room. And I am sitting in my throne. My throne is fluffy and my dungeon is cold and dirty so the enemies don't like it. Neither do I. So they usually don't battle us. We have a strong army. And that's how I like it. And that's how they like it. My castle is big and nice. And I like it. I am married and very rich. My wife is kind. Her name is Sylvia and I like her and she likes me. The End."*

For background information, Brian's father is a journalist who is frequently away on assignment, his mother is the manager of a franchise restaurant, and he is a middle child.

c) Are learning disabled kids automatically exiled from confidence?

When Hilary finished four years of Resource Room help with me, she was apprehensive about working on her own, even though her other teachers and I assured her that she was ready. Hilary's memories included her rage at her own slow progress, her loathing for other kids who skimmed right along, her battles with letters and words until truce and victory opened a kingdom to her, and her unspoken fear that what she had learned might vanish and that she would have to start all over again. She remembered the courage and comfort she had drawn from being with animals, particularly a horse who was boarded in a barn at the end of her road. She used to go there after school, help with the chores, nuzzle the horse's neck, and pour out her troubles. In January of fifth grade — Hilary's first year without extra support — she left this story on my desk.

To a very special person. I write you this story.

There once was a pony that could not trot, and she tried and tried to trot until one day she could trot. After she could trot, of course, she wanted to canter because nothing was good enough for her. One day she could canter just as well as the rest and just as fast. BUT...all the others could jump. She gave up until an old horse that everybody loved told her she could jump just as well as the rest, but she said, "I am too small to do so well, and I will fail." "No" said the horse, "You are better than that. Try, Pony, try." So the Pony did, yet she was not the best and not the worst but the thing was she could do it.

Dear Special V,

I am doing well and I really miss you. I got C, C, C+, C+, and that is the average. See, I was nothing to worry about, and I don't get in fights in the hall!

Love,

Hilary

In the same general category, but younger and a boy, Alexander is a second grader with high intelligence, vast knowledge, innate curiosity, and yet very weak mechanical skills. Consequently, he is in the bottom reading group, the "Hawks." One early fall day, I sat down beside him, and thinking he might have forgotten my name over the summer, I said, "Hi, Alexander, I'm Mrs. Vail." In his bass voice, he said, "I know. I'm Alexander." Putting on a fake pout, I answered, "I know." His eyes lit up, he pointed his index finger right at me, and said, "But, I bet you don't know what it means!" I had to admit he was right. With that, this boy who struggles with the mechanics of school work put his shoulders back, raised his chin, expanded his chest and — proud as any general at a victory — said, "It means brave chief, leader of people, helper and defender of humankind!" Then, he stopped, pointed his finger at me again, and finished, "And, that's true you know. My parents tell it to me all the time."

Boston linguist Anthony Bashir says, "We become the story of who we tell ourselves we are."

d) Does confidence make people stuck-up?

By any measure, Daphne is gifted. Sensitive, literate, athletic, compassionate, and humorous, she bubbles to the top wherever she goes. When she was in sixth grade, she and her classmates read selections from Walt Whitman's *Song of Myself*. Her mother and father read it too, and they each — classmates, teachers, and parents — wrote entries for a new Song of Ourselves. This is Daphne's:

> *Come dance with me*
> *For I love celebrations*
> *To dance the jig of freedom*
> *I am sharing with you.*
> *Like a wild tiger*
> *I race through the fields of life*
> *But at times I stumble*
> *For the field is full of holes*
> *But that doesn't mean I can't walk*
> *Or run...*
> *But no one can escape*
> *And win the race*
> *Without a scraped up knee.*
> *Breathless, I slow down*
> *And step among*
> *The damp grasses*
> *I feel the desire to collapse*
> *But then I realize*
> *I must not stop*
> *For there is no end*
> *To how far I have to go.*

Listen, too, to tidy Elizabeth. She memorizes well, her handwriting is neat, she recognizes sight words through fourth grade level, she works methodically, slowly, accurately. She is more comfortable with reciting than with thinking, and has an IQ slightly below the national norm. She passes her spelling tests, remembers to do her homework, and is diligent with the worksheets in her folder. She waits her turn for corrections at the teacher's desk and doesn't make trouble. She is faithful about her chore of emptying the wastebaskets at home, and every day at school she delivers the attendance sheet to the front office. Asked as a homework assignment to "Write Four Good Things About Yourself," she produced, *"I am nice to people. People like me. I keep my promises. My parents say that I am very kind."*

Marco is a tiny, shiny fifth grader, and the oldest child in his family. In his early school years, he was the champion speller and won the Math Facts Round the World Speed Tournament. He knows the capitals of all the states, and he has never missed the honor roll. His mother and father are working to polish their English. His mother calls him "my perfect boy," and says her pride in him keeps her going through the rough times of settling in a new situation. She says with relief and pride, "You always get everything right."

Marco's reading teacher wants her students to start thinking about inference and those subtle aspects of reading comprehension which are entirely appropriate for this age and grade. Marco is clearly very bright, but he is not reaching out intellectually. He has become a prisoner of his own achievements. Rather than being rungs on a ladder of ascent, his high marks and perfect scores have become the upright posts of a stockade fence, penning him inside the ring of correct answers. His two most frequent questions to his teachers are: "Is this right?" and "Did I get the highest score?"

Of these children, whose confidence is in jeopardy? Is it learning disabled Hilary or Alexander, Penelope the intellectually powerful ghetto dweller, low I.Q. Elizabeth, or Brian — the middle child whose father is frequently absent? No. It is Marco, whose job is to maintain the family honor through academic achievement, and who has no legitimate access to the error half of trial and error, which is, of course, a seedbed of discovery and confidence.

What happens when confidence is jeopardized or extinguished? Living loses its luster and learning loses its joy. The power of negatives and positives is enough to alter the entire course of a human life. The next two sections — which offer specific suggestions — come with the hope that the reader will tie into the underlying purpose of the suggestions and devise additional originals.

Ten Tips for Moms, Dads, Nannies, Grannies, Grandfathers, Teachers, and Other Concerned Adults

1. Just like their peers, confident children need care and attention from adults, and social/emotional, aesthetic, intellectual nourishments. They mustn't be cast loose to forage on their own — in effect, penalized for their own successes.

2. Praise the product or the process, not the person. "I really like the way you practiced over the hard parts of that sonata, so now the whole piece is fluid," as opposed to "You're so talented."

3. The adults' job is to find or create showcases for the young person's talent. As mentioned on page 32, depend on the talent instead of simply praising it. Keep admiration honest by needing what the young person can do. Kids value what is earned over what is bestowed.

4. Keep the atmosphere buoyant, so the learning child has room to err. Be available as a sounding board, consumer, or test-driver for new ideas, remaining fully aware that some of them will bomb.

5. Be on the alert for friendships that will let the kid stretch, learn, and grow, not simply always be on the top.

6. Create opportunities for children to be givers as well as receivers.

7. Set an example of legitimate pride in one's own accomplishments. Show how to accomplish this without boasting, and avoiding the cloying hypocrisy of false modesty. "I'm really excited about the story I wrote," as opposed to "My story is very well written," or "Oh, that story? I'm not sure it's any good."

8. Competence feeds confidence. Whether it's knowing how to change the oil in the car, how to make a souffle rise, or how to spell the words on this week's spelling list, adults need to help kids acquire a solid complement of basic skills, and ornamental competencies.

9. Confidence isn't always noisy.

10. Bombastic displays of glad-handing often mask deep self-doubt. We must not do children the disservice of being fooled by camouflage or disguises.

Six Specific Activities for Teachers

These are compatible with the guiding principles laid out in Chapter One.

1. *Branching Out.* This involves identifying an area the children already know something about, and then expanding from it. As nerve cells reach out to one another, they expand their connections through what is called "dendritic" growth — a term evocative of trees and their branches. Confident children are eager to reach out, to make connections, and to increase both the reach and the density of their information. Let's see how this might work with a topic as ordinary and mundane as weather, which children learn about from TV as well as being out of doors.

Brainstorm with the children. "What do we already know, and what would we like to find out?" All children will be able to categorize obvious climates: hot, cold, rainy, sunny. Most children have firsthand experience with all of those.

Then, inquire, "What other climates are there that we might have heard about or read about?" The probable results would be arctic (or icy), sandy, the rain forest. Then, ask "What are the elements that make up climate?" The probable answers would be sun, clouds, precipitation, temperature, wind, and the influence of time (seasonal changes), geography (mountain ranges), and natural phenomena such as seasonal storms (monsoons or hurricanes), and one-shot deals (volcanic eruptions).

This exploration lays the groundwork for an endless exploration of similarities and differences. "Let's take the five continents and divide the class into five groups. Each group take a continent, and after we have agreed on a common framework of questions, set out to explore the different regions of our world."

This can bring in mathematics (measurements and probability), map-making (both flat and relief), graphing, the aesthetic dimensions of art work (that which is already in existence and original illustrations by the students), literature, poetry, mythology, drama, and an investigation of how weather influences the sociology and anthropology of different parts of the world.

Individual group members might take on independent investigations of the above, or the class as a whole might limit itself to one continent and the small groups would explore the above topics.

The same underlying principle would work for many other topics. The format doesn't matter. *Branching Out* does. Children who feel knowledgeable about the world beyond their home and school boundaries automatically belong to ever widening communities, which in turn bolsters confidence and encourages further exploration.

2. *Learning Pal.* By mail, by phone, by information highway, or in person, team up the children in one grade in one school with age mates in another school. Let them Share and Compare. What are you learning and studying? What do you enjoy most? What do you enjoy the least? If you heard or read a story you really liked and were asked to report on it, would you choose to a) write about it, b) draw it, c) act it out, d) tell it to others. Which do you like best: memorizing or thinking? What do you think is the best thing about your school? If you were going to design our grade in a school of the future, what would you keep and what would you change? Which of these changes do you think are likely or possible?

These questions are just starters. Confidence grows from being encouraged to develop and articulate opinions. With confidence comes joy; with joy comes zest for new ideas.

A teacher or parent might brainstorm more questions from the group, or start with — and stick to — these. Perhaps the Learning Pals would tackle one question every two weeks, which would give each one a week to think and answer, and a week to reflect on the pal's point of view — noting similarities and differences. It would be a shame to rush. Remember the R of Rumination whose importance we discussed in Chapter One.

Kids, like adults, are interested in themselves as well as in others. This kind of format legitimizes both self-awareness and curiosity about other people.

3. *Album: Factual and Fictional.* Let each child select four people from a period of history, a field of endeavor (From A-V on page 78 may be helpful), or from literature. Do an age-appropriate biographical study, choose a way to present it, put yourself in that person's shoes, and write a diary page for a week of that person's life. Then, imagine you are introducing the four to each other. Decide what they will like about one another, and what they might argue over. Put on a short skit dramatizing the meeting.

The benefits of this are closely interwoven with the magical combination of confidence and eagerness to learn. Furthermore, the greater the number of other people a person understands and can empathize with, the wider that person's empathy. Empathy for others augments one's own self-acceptance and, therefore, confidence.

4. *Here They Are.* Myths are part of every culture in every time. They act as mirrors of a society, controls on a society, explanations of a society, or they express common longings in a society. Adults interested in this field enjoy reading Joseph Campbell, Mircea Eliade, Sigmund Freud, and Carl Jung. On an adult level, the philosophy, religion, art, and history which can be interpreted through the mythological lenses are dazzling. Children, too, even young ones, can enjoy the same investigation at a more primitive level.

When working with children, I usually start with a collection of myths such as d'Aulaire's *Norse Gods and Giants*, simply reading the stories aloud for the enjoyment of their content and the art work. Then, I would take one character — let's pick Loki — and ask the children what they see as Loki's main characteristic, his *raison d'etre*, his mission. Though they may use different terminology, even little children will quickly come to the central point — that he is a "trickster," a label they will learn easily. In taking this first step, they embark on the identification and recognition of mythic archetypes. Then, I would ask where — in nursery rhyme, in stories heard or read — have they run into other tricksters. Who are they? Is the Joker in Batman a trickster? Who are the tricksters in Star Wars? Are they benevolent or malevolent tricksters? Who benefits from their tricks? Are they funny or frightening?

Then, I would pick another character — let's say Thor — and think about him in the same way. Once we had established a pantheon, with names for the archetypes, I would read aloud a set of myths from another culture, perhaps choosing D'Aulaire's *Greek Myths*. Reminding ourselves of the geographical, climatic, and historical separation of these two cultures, we would look for the trickster and the other archetypes by now familiar to us, making contrasts and comparisons. When myths and characters from these two cultures were sorted and charted, I would move to myths from a totally different time and place, perhaps Africa or China, or perhaps those of the American Indians.

A thrill of recognition, and an extremely deep reverberation of connectedness, come to the child who sees that Loki, Anansi, and Coyote are the same character given different form by different peoples. The recognition that the trickster is part of every culture means that the trickster is part of human nature. This insight can come as a great relief to children who are feeling guilty about thinking up tricks of their own.

As mentioned previously, feeling an integral part of ever-widening circles expands confidence and broadens intellectual horizons.

5. *Step Right In.* As also mentioned previously, children enjoy displaying what they have studied, what they have learned, and what they have created. As they near the end of a unit or a segment of study, they like to pull the threads together. A wonderful way to let them accomplish all the above is to help them create a classroom museum.

Breaking the classroom into areas corresponding to what has been studied, they can display their models, the books they read, weather charts — whatever happens to have been their product. Then, they can invite other classes to come for a visit, give a tour, and explain the artifacts.

For example, in our school the first grade classes studied Africa.

They worked with a big wall map and a table-top relief map, they listened to tapes of African music and drum ceremonies, they learned about African masks and body painting, and they heard and read African myths. One group studied traditional African land and water transportation, another worked on a display of African animals, and another made studies and drawings of such particular geographical features as deserts, mountains, and rivers.

Although the concepts and topics are highly sophisticated, this was a perfect example of making complexities age-appropriate. The art work was clearly that of young children. When they took two days and created their classroom museum — spreading out their pictures, turning desks into exhibit cases complete with labels — the interconnectedness was exciting; and in the faces of the children who were first creating, then displaying, then explaining the various exhibits, there was obvious growth: shoots, buds, blossoms, and fruit. Rooted in competence, confidence came into flower.

6. *Reading Conferences.* As we saw in the brief stories at the start of this chapter, confidence can be found among the gifted, the learning disabled, the child of average to low-average intelligence, or the untroubled learner.

When special considerations co-exist with confidence, adults must reinforce the child's self-esteem as much as possible. Children who fit the above categories need to go over their reading with teachers or parents — ideally both.

They need praise if they are improving their mechanical skills in word recognition or decoding. They need questions and insights if they are rapid, skillful readers who are sharpening their inferential insights. Those who find it difficult to move from fact retrieval and comprehension to locating the main idea need assurance. Remember about breaking down the task. If they are just plain strong students, they need to share their pleasure.

ONE CHILD'S STORY:
Fair-weather Friends

Success builds confidence. Confidence builds success. That's the easy part. Harder to understand and accept is the nasty surprise that success doesn't make people popular. Confident children, usually generous-spirited themselves, wrestle long and hard to make peace with this uncomfortable truth.

My mother used to warn, "Beware the fair-weather friend." She meant someone who ditches out when the going gets tough. This false friend avoids the contagion of misfortune. So far, so good — simply the sunny side of selfishness.

But, the emotions which draw people together...or push them apart...go beyond simple and sunny. The German word "schadenfreude" means the taking of pleasure from another's distress.

Just as schadenfreude means to take *pleasure* from another's *distress*, its fair-weather flip-flop means to take *displeasure* from another's *success*, bringing us closer to the misconception that it's easier for friends to love each other when successes pile up.

Schadenfreude, jealousy, envy: are they the same? No. Schadenfreude is pro-active; jealousy is re-active. Jealousy and envy, sometimes used synonymously, are different. Jealousy is always corrosive and destructive. Envy can be a spur to productive action: "I wish I could speak French like that. I think I'll learn."

Antonia says that when she was in high school, the days on which grades were posted were the loneliest ones of the school year. When the sheets were tacked up, her classmates would wedge in, stretching on tip-toe to squeal, "I passed!" or "Oh, help!" As others linked arms in relief or support, top student Antonia felt tongue-tied and isolated. She has always ached for a real fair-weather friend, one who loves her when she aims for the top and gets there, one who is joyful when the sun shines on her enterprises. She yearns to give that kind of friendship as well as receive it.

As a little girl, Antonia was shy, friendly, accomplished, and often lonely. Younger than her two close-of-an-age sisters by five and seven years, she was virtually of a different generation. She admired them, they looked on her with bemused tolerance, but she was more of a toy than a sibling. With her friends, she was fair-spirited and generous. She was always willing to help another student, and had good times playing with her classmates one at a time. Other children liked coming to her house, and also inviting her over. But, in big groups such as birthday parties, she turned quietly tentative, and her sense of humor went underground.

Good company for herself, she enjoyed a certain amount of solitude. Like many confident people, she had a wide variety of inner resources. But, she was also a young girl, and parts of her longed for cozy companionship.

I remember the first "formal" Antonia and her class attended. Boys, collected at one end of the room, tried to make small talk in the highs and lows of their yo-yo voices. Girls arrived in clusters of day-glow pastels, outward eyes on one another, inward eyes in merciless self-criticism. Antonia arrived alone, slender, and pimple-free — in a silver dress, silver sandals, and a flower-sprigged, silver barette. The other girls punished her elegance and seeming confidence by carving a moat as uncrossable as it was invisible. Yet, these same classmates threw a ring of support around Adelaide later that same evening.

Nervous, plump, and trying to appear casual, Adelaide dropped herself down on a chair...the same one on which the hostess had absent-mindedly left a platter of pizza. To know the feeling of anchovy topping oozing through pink taffeta is to taste humiliation.

Perhaps, there was real kindness in the other girls' attentions to poor Adelaide, possibly even some schadenfreude. And, surely there was relief: the law of averages says only one girl per party will sit in the pizza.

Antonia hoped the hurtful aspects of competition — and the separations it brought — would abate as she grew older, but the perplexities of fair-weather friendship continue past childhood and adolescence. The two-sided ache of fair-weather friendship can be the uninvited bad fairy at the birthday party.

I saw Antonia two weeks ago. She is now a professor at a nationally renowned university. We talked about confidence and competence: how fair-weather friendship which withstands both sunlight and spotlight is a treasure for both giver and receiver, and how fear of fraudulence often gnaws beneath success: "I got here by a lucky accident...", "If they ever found out..." A former friend's resentment confirms the self doubt; a fair-weather friend's delight banishes it. True fair-weather friends can share one another's successes.

"Maybe the laws of human nature consign to each of us a nasty corner where we rejoice over some one else's loss, particularly if it gains us the competitive edge," said Antonia. Then, laughing, she continued, "You know how the remaining hopefuls in the Miss America contest applaud 'Miss 4th Runner-Up.' They beam at her with gratitude, while they smile at each other with plastic encouragement. I mean NOBODY feels threatened by Miss 4th Runner-Up!"

Antonia, still acutely aware of the shortcomings the world doesn't see, and in touch with her own times of loneliness, has trouble understanding that others are intimidated by her. It was then she spoke her pearl of wisdom. "So many people look as though they've got it all together," she said, "and I suppose some do. But, the world doesn't stop to realize the burden placed on confident people: they're not supposed to NEED anything. It's so important to stay in touch with the needy person inside the successful one."

Then, she laughed, albeit ruefully. "I thought I had fair-weather friendship all figured out. But, I forgot my own lesson. Last Saturday, my mail brought catalogues, bills, a wedding invitation, and a letter from a colleague half-way across the country. We've blurted out more professional woes and fears than we might have with nearby friends or co-workers. I've helped her out a bunch of times. I arranged for her to be on the program at some good conferences, and she's really taken hold. I was delighted to put her together with a publisher for her first book. And, I even made myself be glad for her when her project rolled smoothly along, and I suffered through an editorial divorce. Both projects are on track now; her book will be published six months ahead of mine, and though they're on similar subjects, I think they'll complement each other. I'd rather be generous-spirited than be in competition.

"I opened her letter, smiling in anticipation of hearing from her:

Dearest Antonia,

I can't wait to tell you: a big book club has bought my book for what seems a fortune and...

"Oh, help!" Antonia groaned to herself. "Won't I ever be the good person I'd like to think I am?"

Chapter THREE

CHILDREN AND RELUCTANCE

Wasted Chances and Chances to Waste

Draining energy from students' metaphoric batteries, or acting as a resister on the On/Off switch for learning, reluctance undermines and inhibits the force of true intellectual growth.

When I think about reluctance, three voices echo in my head. One calls from my own family dinner table, one from a reading clinic attached to a major hospital in New York, and one from an anecdote about the wits and pundits at The Round Table at the Algonquin Hotel in New York.

First voice: When our youngest child was 4, I served up a bowl of split pea soup. He refused to eat it, making a disgusted face. I said unwisely, "Young man, you will stay at the table until that soup is eaten." Holding my gaze, he countered, "You're not the boss of my body."

Second voice: Dr. Jeannette J. Jansky, director of the Robinson Reading Clinic in New York and legendary for her deep understanding of children, said, "No child will abandon avoidances which are successful."

Third voice: At one time, The Round Table was a gathering place for some of the quickest wits in New York. As competitive with one another as they were clever on their own, they tested one another's mettle constantly. They devised a scheme in which one member of the group, upon sitting down at the table, would be given a single word and would have to invent an aphorism from it. On this particular day, it was Dorothy Parker's turn. She was given the word, "horticulture." Instantly, she retorted, "You can lead a whore to culture, but you can't make her think."

Going back to the pea soup, we are not the bosses of children's bodies. Even though we can require them to sit down, we cannot control what they swallow or how they digest it. Neither can we mandate how they listen, what they watch, or what they are willing to try. Reluctance to explore cuts kids off from new flavors and nourishments.

Similarly, a child will only move beyond successful avoidance when shown an appealing alternative. Children whose academic performance is below their parents' and teachers' expectation levels often receive massive doses of attention — both negative and positive. Bribes, scoldings, threats, pleas, encouragements, and outside testing keep the attention coming in. Children who are starved for attention feast on this concern while pretending to ignore it.

Finally, although we can preach the value of learning, we can not force reluctant children to think. This doesn't mean we give up; it means we have to acknowledge where our power leaves off, and find ways to turn reluctance into eagerness.

Our purpose here is to explore some of the roots and manifestations of reluctance, so we can help students shed its confinement.

Reluctance, as used here, is an umbrella term covering such stances as sadness, fearfulness, shyness, or passivity. Let's take them one by one.

⊖ A child grieving for a departed person — one permanently departed through death, or intermittently departed through separation or divorce — often cannot summon and sustain the concentration needed for learning. Sadness is a silent siphon.

⊖ A fearful child may be reluctant to take either physical or intellectual risks, or both kinds if the habit becomes entrenched. The child who pulls back from physical exploration is usually left in the dust by more adventurous peers. Loneliness begets more reluctance, and reluctance multiplies the isolation.

Recent violent crimes claiming children as victims have reduced a sense of safety among many young children. When children know that another young person has, for instance, been kidnapped from a slumber party at home and killed, or shot to death outside school, those places formerly seen as sanctuaries become perilous. Statistics on crime involving children continue their steady escalation, increasing adults' responsibilities to teach children how to promote their own safety. A sense of knowing what to do augments a sense of control which, in turn, keeps fear at bay and liberates emotional energies for forward motion.

As we will see in this and several other chapters in the book, children who have been overpraised for the correctness of their answers often become fearful of exploring intellectual unknowns. Uptight, they trade the expansiveness of childhood for the confirmation of "getting it right." Aridity of thought is a tinder box for burn-out.

⊖ Shyness is a neurologically and perhaps genetically determined stance, which the child can compensate for but not eliminate. Harvard professor Jerome Kagan, describing 10 to 20% of adults as being shy and tense, says, "...investigators in many laboratories, working with both animals and humans, have implicated sites in the limbic system

...especially the amygdala, hippocampus, and hypothalamus, and the many circuits in which these structures participate...as influencing initial inhibition and restraint to novel or unfamiliar situations."[1]

In school, although the architecture of the building and the layout of the classroom may be familiar, and the other students known by name, each teacher introducing each new concept is asking the student for involvement in novelty. A shy child's initial impulse is to draw away.

Is a child shy in the classroom? This may be because he or she hasn't done the homework and is unprepared, or may be unsure of being able to deliver the goods. Perhaps a subtle learning disability is leeching strength from the child's performance, and vital energy is being misdirected to conceal it. Perhaps the child has met failure, mockery, or humiliation in school and doesn't want to risk it again.

Is a child shy on the playground? Perhaps he or she is poorly coordinated, doesn't know how to join a group, or feels lost in unstructured play time.

Is a child shy at such places as the supermarket? Perhaps he or she doesn't enjoy advances from strangers.

Is a child shy about playdates? Perhaps he or she is afraid of dogs, new baby sitters, or something as simple as a different brand of sandwich bread at others' homes. At home, with another child as a visitor, he or she may have territorial uncertainty, not knowing how or how much to share.

Shyness is a symptom and also a cause of reluctance.

⊖ Passivity. Why does it matter? True learning is highly aggressive. Learners and thinkers are intellectual adventurers. No very interesting discovery has ever been made by a passive explorer. Certainly, some of the sparkliest ideas may pop up in times of mental roaming which aren't physically energetic: taking a shower, lying on the grass watching clouds. But, these invisible rambles, too, are a kind of exploration.

Passivity is maddening. From parents' standpoints, passive school behavior is beyond their control. From a teacher's point of view, a passive student is an immense frustration or — worse — a confirmation of the secret fear that maybe he or she is not a good teacher.

Having visited these stances, we now need to explore some sources of reluctance so as to:

understand them

undermine them

get out from under them

with the Ready, Get Set, Go of active participation.

Four Sources of Reluctance in Intelligent, Seemingly Healthy Students

1) Physical Problems: illness, irritants, or soporifics

2) The Toll of Giftedness: explorers, appeasers, critics

3) The Different Learner in the Regular Classroom: discrepancy

4) Disruptions of Emotional Energy: invisible negative forces

Physical Problems: illness, irritants, or soporifics

Ill children frequently dissipate their emotional as well as their intellectual energies, and may be forced toward dependence rather than autonomy. Their conditions may range from mild allergic reactions to animal dander to minor or serious chronic infection. Some are victims of malnutrition. Some have constant reminders of their illness through such treatments as chemotherapy or radiation, immobilization in a cast, or the constant need to monitor blood sugar and administer insulin.

A child who has required frequent or emergency treatment may learn that survival depends on obedience, being still, lying back, and having health-giving substances put into you — or unhealthy body parts or products removed.

Something as seemingly simple as vulnerability to asthma can undermine a child's feeling of intactness, leading to avoidance of situations which might trigger trouble, such as going to the house of a friend who has a cat.

Naturally, parents of children who must cope with illness try to keep the child out of harm's way. Unless helped to act otherwise, they may unwittingly reinforce self-doubt or the cotton batting of dependency. The child's goal should be self-reliance and autonomy, but parents, teachers, and the children themselves may need wise guidance to find appropriate methods and settings for fostering such growth.

Adults in the reluctant child's life need to rule out the possibilities of low-grade infections. Quite common in children — particularly during cold and flu season — these may include chronic swollen glands, sinus problems, or urinary tract infections. Not serious enough to cause a major rise in temperature, insidious enough to operate without the danger signal of a bright red rash, low-grade infections drain the child's energy level enough that physical presence in school and passive response to learning may be as much as he or she can muster.

Two other physical problems to consider are difficulty in visual acuity and hearing loss. These act as irritants to the would-be learner. A child whose vision isn't crisp may not see the examples on the board, or the writing on the pages of a book may blur. Undetected hearing loss is increasingly common in school-age children. One possible reason may be that as children go to day care or nursery school at earlier and earlier ages, they are exposed to cold and flu germs. Often, what starts as a cold backs around to the child's ear, causing a middle ear infection.

In many instances, the secondary consequence of *otitis media* is hearing loss, which may be on one or both sides, and may be chronic, permanent, fluctuating, or a one-shot deal. The child who doesn't see well has little incentive to read or pay attention to examples on the blackboard. Children with blocked or distorted hearing may watch the stream rushing by but be unable to become part of it. Children who see or hear poorly may appear intellectually passive when in fact they are physically impaired.

Adults should also look into the child's seat location and desk height, the general temperature of the classroom, allergies and medications, circadian rhythms, sleep and nourishment patterns, and family recreational habits. Why?

Seat location offers a make-or-break difference to the student with vision or hearing issues. Desk height makes a child comfortable or uncomfortable. Uncomfortable children wiggle, lose focus, and disengage. Room temperature can be either comfortable, irritating, or sedating. Hot or poorly ventilated classrooms are sleep-inducing.

Allergies can be as distracting and debilitating as low-grade infections. For example, the child with a runny nose caused by allergies may well feel itchy all over, and may also have fluctuating or consistent trouble hearing. For reasons no one has yet pinpointed, the incidence of juvenile allergies is increasing. Medication for allergies frequently induces drowsiness — which may masquerade as passivity — bringing us from illness to irritants and now to soporifics.

Children, as well as adults, have times of the day when they are alert and times when they incline to grogginess. A child who comes to life at mid-morning but not before may appear passive in the opening hours of school.

Sleep and nourishment needs differ from child to child. As more and more children have evening access to TV and VCRs, more and more children are coming to school sleepy. As families are busier, more and more children eat convenience food and come to school without breakfast. These conditions are as widespread among the affluent as they are among the poor. In fact, the Jung Institute has coined the phrase "Affluenza" to describe deprivation among the wealthy.

Children whose families exhibit, permit, or encourage Couch Potato lifestyles see tempting examples of passivity. Reliance on spectator sports, channel surfing on the TV, and hanging out with MTV all emphasize absorbing vs. generating. Habits are hard to break.

All the above behaviors may pass for reluctance and social/emotional or intellectual passivity.

The Toll of Giftedness: explorers, appeasers, critics

Children with extra dimensions to their knowledge and reasoning may be *explorers*, *appeasers*, or *critics*. And, oddly, each may manifest aspects of reluctance.

Explorers enjoy divergent thinking and manipulating patterns. Encouraged, they bring a high level of intellectual and psychological energy to their endeavors. But, active involvement dies when their heightened perceptions are overlooked and fact retrieval is the order of the day. When divergent thinking is sacrificed to convergent curriculum, explorers trade in their boots, ice axes, and pitons for the cloak of anonymity. Asked by his teacher why he didn't speak up more in class, Eric challenged her, "What's the point?"

Appeasers are prisoners of their own perfection. Dependent on high grades and perfect papers to maintain their self-esteem, appeasers dish back expected answers, let well enough alone, and aim for A's. They douse the lights in their eyes. Asked by her friend why she didn't experiment with her new idea in her essay, Audrey said, "I know it was kind of fun, but I wasn't sure Mrs. Dedham would agree with it. My Dad cares a lot about my grade point average."

Student-critics are a new breed. Over-programmed, over-praised, over-indulged, and over-entertained, these children virtually dare the teacher to be exciting. Bright or gifted children whose parents offer a continuous smorgasbord of entertainment, individual lessons (complete with equipment and chauffeuring), and applause often develop a sense of entitlement which ill suits them for rolling up their sleeves and getting to work. We will see more about this in an ensuing chapter, Children on Pedestals.

In addition, children who have a barrage of lessons at home or after school in such areas as math enrichment, computers, story writing, and instrumental music are using traditionally recreational time for academically oriented activities. Because they are smart (or gifted), they know how to turn the tables. They use school time for socializing.

They chat, whisper, doodle, disrupt, and generally flex those social muscles which otherwise don't get exercise. This behavior can masquerade as academic reluctance. Jody used to sit far down on her spine, chin on her chest, looking up at her teacher through hooded, half-open eyes. As soon as she had a chance, she would pass a note to her neighbor. Asked for her preferences, she said, "All I like in school is recess, lunch, and sports. I never get to have play dates."

This is the place to mention that some gifted people appear reluctant because they are afraid of their own strengths, which, unleashed, might burst the confines of control, taking possession of the person's life. Adults with carefully calibrated relationships and codes of behavior may fear such surprises.

Additionally, we know that some bright students conceal their powers because they don't want to be different from their classmates. Fearful of the isolation frequently imposed on a "brain," they skirt academic edges and avoid intellectual engagement. This happens in elementary school, middle school, and during adolescence. Recent studies indicate that girls in coeducational schools may be particularly vulnerable to this "light under a bushel" stance.

The Different Learner in the Regular Classroom: discrepancy

The different learner in the regular classroom may experience such a discrepancy between learning style and teaching style that active involvement is out of the question. Or, the student's interests and intellect may be on one level, and the content of the curriculum on another. When the student's level is high and the curriculum's is low, boredom is inevitable. Boredom and reluctance prompt the same body English. Equally, if the content of the curriculum is beyond the student's capacity, the result will be frustration or discouragement. These, too, can masquerade as reluctance: "I give up."

The different learner may carry a potentially devastating discrepancy inside. For example, suppose a student with a minor weakness in remembering verbal instructions and explanations also has a minor weakness in handwriting. These two together may form what Mel Levine calls a "lethal cluster." When such a student has a teacher who asks students to copy examples from the board while listening to an explanation, the student is stacked for failure. Mental circuits blow, gears lock, anxiety dilutes memory, skills evaporate.

This is the place to mention Developmental Output Failure Syndrome (DOFS), which, although it afflicts pre-adolescent children, has its roots in the early years of school. Students who don't develop comfortable handwriting in the early years find that their fingers don't keep pace with their minds when their ideas begin to flood. Either their handwriting sprawls illegibly, or perhaps their spelling reverts to primitive levels, the organization of their thoughts is chaotic, or the appearance of their papers conveys an impression of sloppiness and poor attitude. Their papers are returned to them covered with red slash marks — humiliating and discouraging. Mark said "I don't know why I even bother to try. All I ever get back is 'bleeding beasts.'"

Dr. Levine reminds us that the governing agenda of middle school students is "the avoidance of humiliation at all costs." Pretty soon, the intelligent student who faces humiliation in written assignments stops handing them in, leaves them on the bus, dodges and avoids — preferring the teacher's rage or punishments to humiliation in front of his peers.

What starts as avoidance of written output spreads into a reluctance to join classroom discussions, an unwillingness to share ideas, and a general shut-down of output. Once entrenched, this problem is tenacious. But, prevention is simple. Early teaching, continued monitoring, and reinforcement of handwriting skills can kill the roots of DOFS. (*Smart Kids With School Problems* explores handwriting issues in considerable detail.) DOFS is an overt expression of reluctance.

Different learners in regular classrooms often adopt what I would call passive "upsmanship:" they give up in school, cut up in class and at home, and end up in trouble.

Disruptions of Emotional Energy: invisible negative forces

In June, when I open our summer cottage, I get out the flashlights (one apiece for the four bedrooms, the kitchen, and the cellar), which have spent the winter on the closet shelf. Lined up, they all look fine, but when I try them, I find some give no light, some flicker, some are strong, some seem OK at first but then fade. Looking inside, I may find one has a weak bulb, one might have batteries with negative and positive poles misaligned, one switch may have grown rusty, one may have corroded batteries, one may just not have its lid screwed on properly, and one may be in perfect condition — ready to give light. The rechargeable one needs to go to the power source, and will need frequent visits.

The same may be said of many children coping with the realities of today's living. Their external appearances give no cause for concern, but inside they experience disruptions of emotional energy. Because of their metaphoric bulbs, batteries, switches, or limited capacities to store power, they can't shed light on the learning opportunities at hand.

We need to explore seven such disruptions here, seeing their relationship to reluctance.

1. *Depletion.* I was introduced to this topic at a conference roughly twenty years ago. As the speaker explained depletion to us, I felt as if she was drawing a life-size portrait of a child I had been trying unsuccessfully to reach and teach. Talk about virtual reality! The child was there beside me in the

room. In passing on what I learned that day to other teachers and parents, I have seen similar recognition light their faces.

When a child suffers a trauma — losing a parent to death, losing a parent to the part-time death of separation and divorce, losing a place in birth order to a baby sibling, moving from one community (or even house) to another, losing a friend in a fight, losing a pet to death, or losing one's image of one's own self to unexpected failure or success — the trauma leaves a hole. The child remembers previous feelings of completeness and suffers the ache of what has been taken away. Unconsciously, the child reasons, "I remember what I felt like before 'it' happened. I know what the hole feels like now. I can't risk having that hole getting any bigger or — God forbid — having another new hole, so I had better protect everything that's inside of me. I need to keep what I care about under lock and key."

In this effort to stave off the pain of additional loss, the child hoards both feelings and ideas. Mistakenly thinking that each person has only a finite number of ideas, the child keeps them inside — under strict guard. It takes leadership from a sensitive adult to show the child that ideas multiply from being expressed, that feelings bloom when shared, that misers impoverish themselves.

2. Learned Helplessness. In 1975, Martin E.P. Seligman, an Associate Professor of Psychology and Psychology in Psychiatry at the University of Pennsylvania, coined the term "Learned Helplessness" to describe the feelings of powerlessness which are destructive in themselves, and may malevolently expand into clinical depression.

Seligman separated a group of rats into two colonies. He took rats from colony #1 and threw them into a tub of water. The animals thrashed and flailed in efforts to save themselves. While they were still struggling, Seligman reached into the tank and rescued them. These creatures associated their salvation with their own efforts. They inferred that the "locus of control" was inside of them.

Seligman did the same thing with rats from colony #2, but waited until they had given up and were drowning before rescuing them. These animals learned from experience that their own efforts were worthless, and that the locus of control was beyond them.

Then, Seligman repeated the exercises. Rats from colony #1, owners of the locus of control, tried even harder to stay afloat — redoubling their efforts and thinking of new ways to bob and breathe. Rats from colony #2 made a few feeble attempts to survive, gave up, and sank. Experience had taught these rats the lesson of learned helplessness.

It's not such a far cry from Seligman's water tank to some of the mainstream classrooms in today's schools. Most students whose experience has taught them that the locus of control is in the all-powerful parent, teacher, or administrator do not develop the stamina to persist in the face of difficulty. What Seligman calls their "explanatory style" tells them they failed because they are no good, because they are stupid, because the teacher doesn't like them, or because school is a lousy, rotten place anyway. Learned helplessness and reluctance together make a double drain on emotional energy.

3. *Depression.* Diagnosis of depression can only be made by a medical doctor, and the focus of this book is not on pathology. Nevertheless, concerned adults need to be on the lookout, remembering that clinical depression is seriously undetected and undiagnosed in school age children. We may find it in at least two seemingly opposite stances — passivity and hyperactivity.

Depressed passive children do not determine their own course; they are carried along by the current. Uninvolved, seldom disruptive, they may not call attention to themselves either at home or at school. Because listlessness sometimes conceals sadness, adults need to raise their "index of suspicion," looking beyond the convenience of a quiet child to what lies behind compliance.

Paradoxically, depression sometimes masks itself as hyperactivity and lack of focus. (One term in common usage these days is Attention Deficit Disorder with or without hyperactivity — ADD or ADHD — another diagnosis which may ONLY properly be made by a medical doctor.) In this guise, depression removes usual restraints. In contradiction to the withdrawn behaviors generally associated with depression, the child may call out, intrude, push, lose concentration, and forget what he or she is supposed to memorize. We can think of this noisy, disruptive, destructive energy as reluctance turned inside out. Oddly, ADD and depression may cause similar symptoms from opposite etiologies.

4. *Passive Aggression.* Passive-aggressive behavior is a mantle of blamelessness. Withholding, withdrawing, and inhibiting the expression of ideas, feelings, or pleasure are ways of striking out without getting caught in the act of hitting. We all know people who feud politely, going through the manners of their days, "forgetting" the warmths, kindnesses, and appreciations which give life its glow.

Children, too, use this weapon in power struggles over toilet training, eating, sleeping, studying, or reaching out to new experiences and relationships with others. NOT doing, NOT being, NOT trying, NOT risking, NOT enjoying, "forgetting," or having things happen "by mistake" is how a small, seemingly powerless person can drive larger people bananas. Of course, all children do each and all of the above from time to time. Frequency is the tip-off.

5. *Overplacement*. When children are placed in grades for which they are developmentally unready, reluctance is self-protection. Rather than trying and failing, the child who withdraws can't fail. The danger is that avoidance becomes a mask the child cannot remove, and, consequently, he or she goes through life glued into a costume. Incorrect grade placement is a particular hazard among the verbally precocious and the genuinely gifted. Because there are so many things these children can say, read, factor, or discuss, the adult world is sometimes snookered into assuming overall readiness for accelerated standing.

Incorrect grade placement has also caused the needless destruction of eager, intelligent, potentially successful children whose start of schooling (and choice of grade level) is governed purely by their birthdates and their school's cut-off policies. Many of these children are boys, many have summer birthdays. Many have been brutally injured by adults' automatic adherence to numbers on calendars. Jim Grant, who focuses on developmental issues, mockingly talks of reliance on "wax volume certification for school readiness." The wax volume comes from the number of candles blown out on the child's birthday cake. Chronological age is only one of four determining factors in sophisticated, individually tailored grade placement, the others being intellectual development, social/emotional development, and overall developmental level.

Neglected developmental needs fester, creating problems in learning.

6. *Hidden Disability*. An undetected, unacknowledged, or misunderstood learning disability inter-

rupts the smooth flow of emotional energies with erratic pulsing of hesitancies and surges. Children who are confused by — or ashamed of — their inability to do what their peers do easily often take a reluctant stance to avoid exposure. *Smart Kids With School Problems* addresses this point in detail.

7. *Genuine Boredom.* Gifted children crave opportunities to exercise their imaginations. Divergent thinkers need open-ended questions and are genuinely bored by convergent curriculum. Arabella said, "I feel like cake frosting being squeezed through the slot at the end of a pastry decoration tube."

The Get Ready of Arousal, the Get Set of Attention, the Go of Action

Get Ready. Arousal comes first. We need to check out the physical systems discussed earlier in the chapter to insure that this capacity is intact. Then, we need to remember that emotions have either an energizing or a dampening effect on the student's availability.

Get Set. Students pay attention to interesting ideas and activities. Wise adults find ways to join the familiar and well-loved with the newly required. At home or at school, the sports enthusiast who is afraid of math can put the two together charting averages, keeping running records of scores, comparing one team's statistics with another's. Wise parents and teachers also open the introduction of a new concept with a discussion of what the children know already.

Go. Activities which honor originality over conformity, and which join children's ideas with their own physical and emotional experiences, will prompt the Go of action.

In her book, *Engaging Children's Minds*, Lillian Katz distinguishes active learning goals from perfect-performance goals. It goes without saying that active learning is not limited to school.

Active learning asks, "How much can you do with this? How far can you go?" Perfect-performance asks, "How well can you do?"

When parents overemphasize grades and when teachers set perfect-performance goals, kids worry, "Do I have (know) enough to do this?" When parents and teachers set learning goals, kids say, "What can I do?"

When the emphasis is on perfect performance, kids worry how they will be judged. Kids in trouble give up, saying, "I'm bad at this." When the emphasis is on learning, kids are absorbed by competence as they develop flexible strategies.

When the learning environment emphasizes perfect-performance goals, kids take pleasure in others' failures. When the learning environment emphasizes learning goals, kids become magnanimous.

The cumulative effect of pressure for perfect performance is for children to distance themselves from institutional learning, and from the capacity to lose themselves independently in ideas or topics.

At home as well as at school, the main purpose of education is to cultivate in the learner the disposition to keep on learning. We serve this purpose best when we shift from the notion of delivery by the adults to the idea of activity by the children.

Ten Tips for Moms, Dads, Nannies, Grannies, Grandfathers, Teachers, and Other Concerned Adults

1. Autonomy will vanquish reluctance. Create situations in which the child is in charge.

2. Being quiet is not necessarily the same as being reluctant. Some children are thinking aggressively while reading or writing. Look for what's inside the body English.

3. Reluctant children can be lured into active stances through humor.

4. The simple act of putting on a costume hat can help a child assume a whole new identity. Having a laundry basket of hats, capes, and shirts readily accessible can release the child's anaesthetized sense of adventure.

5. Children unwilling (or afraid) to express their own emotions will frequently be very outspoken through the voice of a puppet. A supply of store-bought people and animal puppets can be a funnel for feelings and ideas. Or, let the children make their own from socks or brown paper lunch bags.

6. Group singing elicits active participation from the members without the embarrassment or fear of individual attention. At home or at school, learning a song, expanding the number of verses, or making up new verses can be an opportunity for a child to feel the contagion of active involvement.

7. Memorizing poetry as a group, family, or school confers immediate membership. Recitation provides automatic shared experience. The selections can be long or short, depending on age and stamina. One family learned *The Cremation of Sam McGee* and would recite it at all family events, and during long car, train, or bus trips.

8. Simple crafts projects give children concrete evidence of their ability to create. Be it a potholder from a toy loom, a lariat from plastic strips, or Creepy Crawlers from a mold, even children who are not particularly artistic can produce an object.

9. Mysterious or humorous story starters can tempt children's imaginations. "I was sitting there minding my own business, when I heard a creaking and groaning from the stairs. I thought I was the only one in the building, but..."

10. Knowing a few magic tricks gives a child a sense of power and surprise, two feelings which obliterate reluctance.

The precepts above, combined with the Six Specific Activities For Teachers to follow, will help the reluctant learner become an active enthusiast.

Six Specific Activities for Teachers

While the following activities are suggested with sad, fearful, shy, or passive children in mind, they are suitable for all children in a class. Some will be fascinated, others mildly interested, and, sadly, some will make pedantic use of exciting opportunities.

1. *High Fives.* People are interested in their own reactions and in themselves. (Don't you peek at your chart in the doctor's office?) Even children whose reluctant stance indicates a lack of interest in exploring the outside world are interested in their own thoughts. We can tap into this natural curiosity by helping them identify the five senses. Then, give each student twenty index cards — four apiece for each of the five senses. If you do this in the fall, ask the students to think of the things they see in the fall. Write or draw those ideas on one card. On the next, write or draw sounds one hears in the fall. On the next, chart or indicate special fall smells; on the next, special fall textures and touch sensations; and on the fifth, special fall tastes and flavors. Follow the same procedure with the next group of five cards, moving to sights, sounds, smells, touches, and tastes of winter. Do the same for spring, and the same for summer. Give each student a notebook ring, a punch, and two more cards for front and back covers, and there they have a collection of their own bodily experiences to draw from in their ongoing work.

Then, ask them to choose one — perhaps a winter sight — and write or draw an elaboration. Post the results on the wall of the classroom or on the refrigerator at home, or both!

The very act of joining physical perception, emotional reaction, and bodily experience quickens emotional energies, dislodging reluctance.

2. *Letter to the Editor.* Find an area the child is interested in. Do this by observing what makes him or her laugh, cry, or sit forward, instead of by asking, "What are you interested in?" That's too easy to answer with "Nothing," or the reluctant student's classic response, "I don't know." When you see what topics or ideas engage the child's emotional energy, say something like, "I can tell you think it's important to recycle...or it's scary to find yourself left at the mall...or that it's funny to see grown-ups put on Halloween costumes. For your homework for the next three nights, I want you to start, polish, and produce a letter to the editor of the local newspaper, explaining why you feel as you do. I'll help you send it or deliver it. If the paper doesn't publish it, we'll publish it here in school."

If this is a home project, change the wording but keep the idea.

Personal involvement in situations and ideas creates a conduit for parallel engagement in learning.

3. *From A to V.* Using alphabetical order, list possible avocations and vocations. This can be done by a whole class, by a family, by a small group in school, or as a solo activity.

The list might include author, bassoonist, cartoonist, diver, explorer, fish keeper, handyman. The point is to include both hobbies and livelihoods. Encourage activities from as wide a range as possible. Howard Gardner's seven intelligences (logical/mathematical, linguistic, musical, spatial, bodily-kinesthetic, interpersonal, and intrapersonal) make a good organizational grid.

Then, ask each child to finish the sentence, "I have the natural ability and interest to become..." Don't limit the choices to one, any more than we would limit the number of possibilities per letter to one. The point is to generate a variety and help the children visualize themselves in various roles, attaching the natural power of "explanatory style" we saw earlier to specific, personal visions which may become plans. They should write about or illustrate themselves in their chosen vocations or avocations — the latter being given noble status, please.

The opportunity to choose — and to match oneself to — exciting opportunities point the child toward those possibilities which convert reluctance into involvement.

4. *The Same Story.* Pick a folk tale. For example, let's use *Belling the Cat*, in which the frightened mice hold a council to decide how to protect themselves against their foe — a busy, feline marauder. After many suggestions and deliberations, the little tribe decides that if the cat wore a bell, they would all have warning of an approach. They all agreed that this was the perfect solution and set about rejoicing, until one brave and thoughtful mouse asked who would put the bell on the cat. Either write the story out, let each child write it out and compare versions, or draw a story board. Enjoy and discuss the story. Then, ask each child to use the same issue in a contemporary story — one about life at school, on the block, or at home.

To discover the link between old-fashioned stories, personal concerns, and modern living is to bring an immediacy to reading that most children cannot resist. This, in turn, changes the reluctant or surface reader into an engaged thinker.

5. *From Start to Middle.* Ask the child to pick an area of study or enjoyment for a portfolio. Explain that the purpose is NOT to have an album of perfection, but rather a record of growth. Note that the title is Start to Middle, not Start to Finish. All of us need to continue to grow and to expand our competencies over our lifetimes. While it is deeply satisfying to finish a project — a book, for example — an author hopes never to have finished learning how to write better.

Save the first endeavor, add to the file as the student's competence grows, and at the end of a pre-decided amount of time — six weeks or six months — review with the child what has changed. Ask the child to explain what was hard, what was easy, how learning happened. Transcribe the comments and attach them to the portfolio. A tangible record of actual growth is incontrovertible evidence of success, something the passive child needs to taste.

6. *Be a Sport.* Laughter is active, not passive. Many atypical learners draw away from reading and writing because their basic decoding and encoding skills are not solid. We need to offer drill mixed with laughter. *Be a Sport* can be done on beginning or intermediate levels.

For beginners, take three containers. In the first, put slips of paper with consonants, or consonant blends typically found at the beginning of words, such as *sp*, *st*, *tr*, *bl*, etc. In the second container, put slips of paper with vowels or vowel teams, such as *ai*, *ea*, *ee*, *oa*. In the third container, put slips of paper showing single consonants or consonant pairs typically found at the end of words, such as *rd*, *rt*, *st*, *nd*, etc. Then, ask each child to pick one slip of paper from each container and put the sounds together to make a nonsense word. If a real word comes up by chance, the child should try again. Once the nonsense word is formed, it becomes the name of a sport, and the child must invent from imagination what kind of a sport it is and how it is played. Is it for two players, for teams, does it use a ball, a frisbee, a Martian implement — how is it scored, is it enjoyable, what age is it for?

For intermediates, use two or three containers. The first holds slips of paper showing consonant-vowel-consonant (cvc) syllables such as *jup*, *pib*, *lof*, *zat*, or *feg*. The second shows more cvc syllables, including some common suffixes such as *ment*, *less*, *able*. The child draws a slip from each container, and, again, makes a nonsense word. If three containers are used, the first might contain closed syllables, consonant-vowel-consonant, such as the ones listed above. The next might contain open syllables such as *go*, *li*, *va*, *ne*, *hu*. The final container would hold slips with cvc syllables and common suffixes such as those listed above. The resulting words might be "Pib-less" or "Lof-li-ment." Then, the student describes the imaginary game. Illustrations are always welcome, entertaining, and tempt children to join their mind's eye to the mind's ear in the music of words.

The active stance of imaginative, original humor exemplifies the benevolent weaponry we can use against reluctance.

ONE CHILD'S STORY
"Birdbrain"

Marnie turned 8 on September 14, a week after entering third grade.

Ellen, her mother, tends to be a worrier and is often tired from taking care of Marnie and her little brother. Marnie's father, Phil, travels frequently on business, so the major share of child-raising responsibility falls to Ellen.

Marnie was a full-term baby, neither the pregnancy nor the delivery were unusual, she met her major developmental milestones on time, but was always a physically cautious child. Ellen remarked to the pediatrician that the child liked to size situations up before jumping in, that she would watch from the sidelines — seeming to assess the risks, that she moved rather stiffly, and, for instance, was quite clumsy in chasing a ball. The physician said that since she was within normal limits, he saw no reason for concern. Ellen was delighted, because she needed the reassurance that she was doing a good job.

Marnie's first year was uneventful. She smiled frequently, enjoyed people both old and young, and in spite of being physically cautious, learned to sit, stand, crawl, feed herself, and begin to walk. She understood what was said to her, and her mother read stories and sang songs. She loved being cuddled by her mother, relatives, or other adults.

Between the ages of 1 and 2, she enjoyed the simple activities in the twice-weekly play group her mother arranged. Her parallel play was entirely appropriate, she walked steadily and began to run (gingerly), and her receptive and expressive language capacities were very strong. She loved to sing.

Between the ages of 2 and 3, she was quite fearful of imaginary creatures: ghosts, goblins, and a giant with a Punk hairdo she said lived in the coat closet. She insisted on a night light. She learned to stay dry without much trouble, but bowel control was another matter. Her mother couldn't tell whether she was rebellious, whether she didn't sense the warning signals, or whether she just didn't care.

During this year, she began to draw back from playing with active children and was fearful of rough play or physical jostling. In such situations, she would suddenly be extremely busy with a toy, a book, or would concoct some tale or information about a farm. She had picture books about farms, a Fisher Price farm set, and she herself would often become a horse or cow. Sometimes, when she was tired or upset, particularly at the end of the day, she would go to a little spot under the stairs, which would become a barn. She would rock and pat herself, making up little songs about animals. Her mother would find her there with soiled pants.

Between the ages of 3 and 4, Marnie was imaginative, sensitive, verbal, loving, and continued being physically timid. Bowel control was still a problem, but again the pediatrician said not to worry, and Ellen was relieved to get off the guilt hook. Marnie went to nursery school four mornings a week, and the teacher's reports held no surprises.

Phip, Marnie's baby brother, was born just after Valentine's Day, the winter Marnie was 4. She was nicely settled in nursery school, had made a few neighborhood friends, and although she still avoided physical challenge, her teachers found other ways for her to interact with her classmates. She seemed very proud to have a brother, gave the baby some toys she had outgrown, and was surprised but not annoyed when he didn't know how to enjoy them. Phip smiled at her, for her, with her. He would light up when she came into view. Things seemed to be solid in spite of the big change. But, there was still a problem with bowel control.

The year she was 5, her nursery school teacher remarked that she seemed to be more of a watcher than a doer, and she was reluctant to try new activities (academic or extracurricular) unless they involved books. She was a self-taught, strong sight-reader, and she could play simple math games in her head.

On the playground, she was "Miss Quality Control," keeping watch and reporting to the teacher when anyone did anything wrong. In the dress-up corner, she would become a farm mother; in the block corner she would build barns and pastures. Her favorite song was Old MacDonald. As part of the standard procedure in her school district, Marnie was given an I.Q. test, which showed very high verbal scores — and performance scores only in the average range. In spite of this discrepancy, she was pronounced gifted, and slated to receive extra attention and possible acceleration.

For Marnie's 6th birthday, her mother took her with two neighborhood friends on an hour's journey to the North Country Nature Museum, which has a small working farm. She was in paradise! She studied everything — quietly, passionately, reverently — putting out the tip of her index finger to touch, and smiling with deep pleasure. Afterwards, she memorized the souvenir booklet, knew the layout of the grounds as if she had been the architect, and would sink into reverie about the experience.

That year in school was terribly difficult. Because of her high verbal I.Q., and because she was a fluent reader, the school placed her in a group of children who were a year to a year-and-a-half older. She made the September 15 cut-off date for school entrance by one day, and the administrator said, "Somebody's got to be the youngest, and she's so smart, if we don't put her ahead, she'll be bored."

At home, Phip was charming the man in the street and everyone else who came near him. Bewitchingly handsome, outgoing, and fearless, he would crow with delight at any opportunity to climb, reach, stretch, roll, listen, babble, sing. During this time, Marnie's father was sent on a three-month assignment to another country, and her mother bought a computer to use for writing articles she hoped to sell, for keeping household records, and for a volunteer project she had undertaken for a neighborhood cause. Ellen was busy learning her new machine and was absorbed in her work.

At school, Marnie was afraid of the bigger children, particularly boys. They would say they were going to chase her and put her in a dungeon. Just the mention would make her fearful. She wouldn't want to go out on the playground, and would beg to stay inside and play farm or read. When she did go out, chances were the others were too busy to notice her, but apprehension stained her time. Occasionally, she soiled her pants in school.

For the first time, her teacher used the word "passive." The teachers, along with Ellen and Phil, agreed that she should have been placed with the group a year younger, and plans were made to readjust the following September.

In spite of the difficulties, two good things happened that year. First, her aunt and uncle invited her for a week-long visit with them and their children. When she arrived, a brand new two-wheeler was waiting for her. They didn't give her any choice: "Bike time for everybody." Before she could say, "I don't want to," she was wearing her new helmet and being pushed from behind by her uncle. She learned well, and by the end of two days was riding back and forth, around corners, and braking on the hill. However, when invited to return several months later, she cried and said she didn't want to go.

Second, that spring, there was a large family gathering at a compound of cabins in the mountains. As the big group was gathering in the central building one evening, someone noticed that a bird had gotten in and was in a swooping panic to escape. The other children squealed and shrieked, the mothers covered their heads, the fathers talked heroically about tennis rackets and big towels. Marnie took a piece of bread, climbed up on a high stool, and quietly held out her hand. The bird saw, circled, and landed. Marnie stroked the frightened creature with her free hand, speaking gently and soothingly, and walked to the door. The bird stayed on her hand for several minutes, cocking his head and looking at the little girl. Then, off he flew.

The other children were awe stricken. "How did you know what to do?" "How come he came on your hand like that?" "How come he wasn't scared of you?" "Where did you learn to do that?" Marnie answered, "I didn't learn it anywhere. I just tried." She was quiet and very proud. One cousin, a boy she had been particularly afraid of, looked at her and said with obvious admiration and affection, "Good going, Birdbrain!" A nickname — that badge of belonging — was born. The formerly feared cousins had become her friends and admirers, and will doubtless call her Birdbrain all her life.

That winter, Marnie's agemates learned to skate — an important activity in her upstate New York community, where girls could choose either figure skating or hockey. Most children skated on both Saturday and Sunday. Marnie didn't...wouldn't...couldn't...get the knack. She had intermittent trouble with soiling, and was resistant and anxious.

She transferred her farm passion to Trolls, and was only comfortable in small situations where nothing unexpected would happen. Instead of resenting or hitting out at Phip, she seemed to regress to his level and was totally happy playing with him and his friends.

In school, she began avoiding her work. Her teacher said, "Marnie just isn't getting anything done. Her mental math is fine, but her written arithmetic is weak. She 'loses' her phonics sheets, even though she reads well.

"She's also taking a lot of "in-house field-trips:" to the nurse, the bathroom, the water fountain. She doesn't seem to enjoy art, and we know how she feels about gym. But, I'm afraid so much effort is going into avoidance, that she has very little left over for forward motion. I don't feel as if I'm reaching this child. I think she's kind of shutting down, and I don't know how to get her going. Whenever it's time to deliver the goods, she drifts off to shadowland."

At a conference including Marnie's teacher, Ellen and Phil, the lower school administrator, and the school psychologist, a five-prong plan was born:

1. Marnie would have a thorough check-up with the pediatrician to rule out any possible physical ailments, as well as the possibility of clinical depression.

2. She would repeat her grade placement, thereby moving to the older end of the group.

3. Her parents would arrange for her to be a "teacher's helper" with Phip's gymnastics group, thereby giving her a "refresher course" in basic body movement and control. The skates would go into the attic, and her parents would arrange to get her to weekend Introduction to Dance classes at a nearby town.

4. She would keep a chart showing Something New I Did Today I Had Never Done Before.

5. Her parents would buy her a hamster, hoping to capitalize on her gentleness with animals and her obvious pride over the Birdbrain incident.

Strategies such as these should give her courage, let her know she is understood and valued, and help her set reluctance aside in favor of that frame of mind which Harvard psychiatrist Ned Hallowell shows us is the foundation for current joy and future engagement:

"Remember that time of life, that state of mind, when you were Lord of all the fields and king or queen of all the stars, and feel now how much your will to love and dream and risk and create depends on your having had that once, having had that time when everything was new and possible and impossible all at once."

Chapter FOUR

CHILDREN AND ANGER

Fires Within

The words "anger" and "danger" are spelled alike but don't rhyme. Should they? Are they psychological cousins?

Every person feels anger at one time or another. We see it in very young babies and among the very elderly, not to mention all of us in between. It's part of human nature. But, when anger is habitual or violent, its heat melts judgment and intellectual balance, and scorches other stabilizing emotions. When it rages out of control, it carries the individual away.

Just as all fire needs to be fed by oxygen, all anger is fueled by emotional energy. Energy used to fuel anger is spent — and therefore unavailable for the forward motion of learning, as we will see in the children of this chapter.

Are there also times when anger is more dangerous in its absence than in its emergence? Repression and control are high-energy efforts. Children who are denying their own anger may have little energy left for learning. Children who must continually try to rein in recurrent anger exhaust their emotional and intellectual powers.

If we explore anger in the metaphor of fire, we see different kinds with varying intensities, durations, and causes.

There is the single, startling flash of the firecracker: one explosion — short-lived — which grabs attention. I saw an example at a fourth grade birthday party. Jeannette ate the candies on Martha's favor basket. In impulsive response, Martha un-capped her Sharpliner pen and popped Jeannette's balloon. One offense, one swift revenge.

There is volcanic fire whose eruption buries people in lava and ash. From afar, the mountain may appear a benevolent landmark; but close at hand, rumbling and smoking, it spews out its deadly flow of molten rock.

Floyd had never learned to read or write. Be-cause he was physically large and generally well-behaved, he was promoted from grade to grade, his reports carrying that free-floating hokum, "He needs to catch up. He should try harder." As his classmates moved from learning letter names and sounds to blending sounds into words, to recogniz-ing sight words, to breaking big words into syllables, to writing stories, and to reading for information and for pleasure, Floyd fell farther and farther be-hind. No, actually he stayed where he was — baseline illiterate — but because his classmates were forging ahead, he appeared to be dropping back-ward. His large, urban school did not provide diag-nostic testing until fifth grade. Although his teach-ers and peers sensed anger in his body English and in some comments he had made, no one antici-pated the power of his imminent eruption.

When he and his class arrived at the art room for their weekly session, the art teacher said, "Today, instead of making things, we're going to read about the lives of famous artists. The books are on the back table. Each of you pick a person and..."

"Not fair," began the rumble from Floyd's throat. Gathering power, Vesuvian, it came again, "Not fair." Louder and more passionately he called out, "That's not fair. This is art class." And then came the full force. "That's not fair. I won't. Not fair!" He extended his arm and with a swift backhand stroke swept the clay figures off the front table onto the floor, smashing them. He lunged for a side table, where more clay student work was on display, and swept those, too, to the floor. By now he was bellowing, "Not fair."

The teacher said, "Floyd, calm down. Stop." But, he didn't hear or didn't respond. He went to the display bookcase, and before anyone could stop him, he swept those figures, too, to the floor — to demolition. The other students drew back in shock...and fear. Floyd was large and physically powerful. Finally, he threw himself at the back table. He swept the books to the floor, by now screaming, "NOT FAIR." When all the books were on the floor, he picked one up and tried to tear the pages out. But, he had too big a handful. As he tried to rip them, a bellow of pain came from his depths — "NOT FAIR!" — and he dropped to the floor and burst into tears, sobbing, shaking, cradling the hated book, and rocking back and forth. "It's not fair."

Every piece of student sculpture, including some of his own finest pieces, lay shattered on the floor — clay dust rising from the devastation like volcanic ash.

The teacher said, "Why did you do such a thing?" Some other kids said, "Hey, that's not fair — what YOU just did." Floyd remained silent until one girl, the smallest kid in the class said, "I'd do it, too, if I couldn't read. Art is the only thing Floyd is good at. He felt safe coming in here until this happened." Floyd got to his feet and ran out of the room.

Spontaneous combustion ignites fires which seem to come from nowhere. Items which are innocuous by themselves are incendiary in combination with other everyday objects.

Damp hay stored in a barn with dry hay loaded on top of it can burn down the barn. The unventilated utility closet in the garage or basement — filled with paint cans, paint thinner, and rags soaked in turpentine — can destroy the garage, the car, and perhaps the house or entire apartment building.

Damp hay needs to be tossed in the air and the sun. Even if they aren't going to be washed, oily rags need to be unwadded, aired, and separated. Grievances kids have with one another also need to be aired. Classrooms and households often contain potentially explosive combinations. But, light and air, circulating around a problem, can usually prevent conflagration.

Timmy and Jonathan are brothers only eleven months apart. Because they were born in the same calendar year, they are in the same grade in school; and because their rural school has a small population, there is only one section per grade level. This means the boys are in the same class with the same teacher, competing for friends in the same pool of peers.

Timmy, the older boy, is reflective, intelligent, and serious. Jonathan is a born politician. Gregarious, daring, funny, and persuasive, he plays the class clown, and his antics often derail discussions of ideas or introductions to new concepts. Timmy is eager for the knowledge to be gained from school. Jonathan sees school as an arena for flexing his social muscles.

Their wise fourth grade teacher has placed them in separate groups for reading, math, and cooperative learning, but, realistically, there are still those times when the whole class must listen or work together. She has found that putting an outline of her presentation on the board or on the overhead projector widens the intellectual scope for Timmy, while also giving Jonathan a preview of where the discussion is heading. This helps him focus, just as it gives

Timmy a chance to think ahead. This simple method has short-circuited much of the potential disruption, because each boy's individual and academic needs are met.

At home, the boys' fighting was worrisome to both parents. The worst conflicts erupted in the bathroom and at the table. If both boys used the same bathroom to get ready for school, toothpaste fights, water fights, pushing, shoving, head dunking, and even fist fights flared. After talking the problem through as a family, the parents offered to share their own bathroom with one boy — one month at a time. Because both adults were early risers, this was not inconvenient. At the end of the month, the boys switched. Each felt privileged. The morning fights stopped. Not only did this make family life more pleasant, the boys no longer arrived at school all burnt out. They were available for learning.

On the same monthly schedule, one boy was in charge of setting the table for supper, clearing the dishes, and getting the table ready for breakfast before going to bed. The other boy was in charge of making the nightly salad, and washing the plates or putting them in the dishwasher. New month, job swap. Their evening energies were free for homework or just plain having fun.

Fires in peat bogs burn hidden under ground. Working little, licking tongues of flame through uncharted labyrinths, peat bog fires are impossible to extinguish because they pop up from seemingly random sources. Some anger works the same way. It is always there, under the surface, traveling through intellectual warrens, burning its way along emotional paths.

Meet Tiffany, 9-years-old. Her parents separated when she was 4, divorced when she was 6, and her father has moved away. Tiffany has an older sister who considers her a pest, and a younger brother whose well-documented learning disability requires massive amounts of tutoring — a considerable drain on the family's available resources of money, time, and attention. Her mother has a new boyfriend, and in the evenings either leaves Tiffany and her brother in the care of her impatient older sister, or entertains her marital prospect at home and wants no interruptions from the children.

Tiffany misses her father dreadfully. He left when she was 4, and some unresolved issues of guilt doubtless feed the flames in the peat bog of Tiffany's soul. She fantasizes about being his favorite if he lived nearby, but in fact he lives at some distance and is increasingly unreliable about staying in touch.

Tiffany is curious about her sister's make-up, cassettes, school books, earrings, t-shirts, friends, shaven legs, and tampons. Sometimes, she sneaks into her sister's room to explore these tokens of maturity. She tries to cover her tracks, but somehow Marcella always knows and finds those ways to punish her that only an older sister really understands. Tiffany is both awed and smoulderingly resentful.

Because of Dan's dyslexia, he gets extra attention from their mother, and Tiffany has to do her homework in the spare room of the tutor's apartment three times a week. This means she misses chances for play dates or for just hanging out with other kids in her neighborhood. Because finances are limited and Dan's tutoring takes precedence, she cannot start ballet lessons. She sometimes wishes she had a learning disability of her own, so people would make excuses for her and give her extras. But, when she thinks seriously about it, she's glad she is good in school and feels sorry for Dan. The fire in these subterranean passages travels in opposite directions simultaneously — moving one way toward resentment and jealousy, and in reverse to the guilt these feelings engender.

Because she is fair-minded, Tiffany sees how hard her mother works, and how she has struggled to keep things decent for herself and her three children. Even though she is a child, Tiffany can muster up genuine pleasure that her mother has such a compatible boyfriend. At the same time, she is a little girl hungry for emotional contact and angry at being emotionally parched.

Two weeks ago, Tiffany decided to run away. She took some of her sister's hairbands and eye shadow, and some of the cash which was sitting in the tutoring envelope. She put on her mother's favorite sweater, put four apples and the picture of her father in her backpack, and left home. After several hours of walking around the city, she was tired and headed back to a park near her apartment. She didn't want to go home, but she was afraid to be too far away. She sat on a bench and ate an apple, watching the children leave the playground. In the twilight, she pulled the sweater closer around her. It smelled of her mother's perfume, and she began to feel very small and very alone.

She thought about the scene at home — the worry over her absence, what they would all be saying about how much they missed her, and how they were frightened. But, then she thought, "They're not nice to me. They take me for granted. They don't even help." These images kept her fires of revenge alive. She began to cry. After all, she was only 9.

Then, from behind, she heard her mother's voice and felt her mother's hands on her head. "Tiff, it's you! Here you are. We were so worried." Her mother was crying. "We've been hunting and calling everywhere. Why did you do this? What's wrong?"

Tiffany tried to explain how she felt left out and angry. "Oh, Tiff, we all love you. We count on YOU to keep us all sane. Come on home now, honey. We'll have something nice and warm to eat."

When they got home, Marcella and Dan gave her big hugs and told her that they loved her, but right after supper, her Mother said, "I've promised to meet George. We won't be out late. You kids have a nice time, O.K.?"

When they were alone, Marcella said, "Give me back my hairbands. I know you've got them in your backpack. And, don't EVER take anything of mine again." Dan said, "I had to miss my lesson all because of you." Tiffany went to bed.

Is it any wonder her teacher had to speak to her over and over the next day? "Tiffany, please pay attention." "Tiffany, you're not listening." Finally, "Pull yourself together, Tiffany. Do I have to move your desk...again?"

Embers can rekindle. Their fire can be brought back to life by bellows, by being stirred, or by having new kindling and logs added on. Gray and often cold-looking, embers camouflage their potential to burn. Similarly, old grievances can shoot forth tongues of new flames. Long-ago hurts rise to new life like a phoenix when the embers of memory are breathed upon, or prodded with a poker, or when a new hurt is added to one which had been thought to be extinguished.

For most of the school year, Arthur and Jed are good friends. When the time comes for the Science Fair, they are both excited and eager. Then, Jed wins first prize again, and again Arthur gets a Commendation Ribbon, as does everyone who enters the contest. Hot flames of jealousy shoot through Arthur, who tries to disguise them. Jed calls and says "Hey, you want to shoot some hoops?" "No." "Tomorrow?" "I don't know. Maybe. Probably not." "What's wrong?" "Nothing." "Well, it can't be nothing if you won't shoot hoops. You always want to shoot hoops." "Well, maybe tomorrow. We'll see."

Arthur tries to leave his embers undisturbed. He wants them to die out, so he can be friends with Jed again. He really wants to shoot hoops and have fun. Finally, he takes a chance, he and Jed have a good time, he figures the problem is solved. And, it is — until the next year, when the same thing happens again.

Forest fires start small, spread, and blaze over large areas. They destroy but also clean the forest of dead wood, and make way for the new growth which is otherwise choked by old trees. Regeneration cannot begin without clearing.

Ben had a very unhappy second, third, and fourth grade in his new school. Leaving a home and neighborhood they loved for what seemed like an excellent business opportunity for his father, he and his parents landed in a different part of the country — far from grandparents, other relatives, and friends — where the customs and even the names for food seemed alien.

Ben's parents had been dazzled by the size of the salary, the exotic sound of where they would be going, and by the chance to leave familiar things and people behind and strike out on their own. The new opportunity made the familiar seem boring. Ben's four grandparents had stayed in the same town all their lives, and had urged their children to "make something of yourself" and "move up in the world."

As Ben and his parents settled in their new location, they tried to be good sports and tell each other things were getting better every day — that they were on an adventure together — but the chipper talk was hollow.

First, their little dog had been terrorized by a neighbor's larger, fierce dog, who had already bitten three people. Ben's parents tried to talk to the dog's owner, who said, "I raise 'em tough, and that's the way I like it."

As a result, they didn't feel comfortable being out of doors. Ben's father's commute was long, and his mother took a job she didn't particularly like just because it was fairly close by.

Ben's class had thirty-two kids and one teacher — a far cry from the seventeen students, a teacher, and an assistant he had before; and because of a budget cut, there was no music teacher. Music had been Ben's favorite subject at his other school.

Because the classes were large, Ben's teachers during those three years kept everyone moving in lock step through the curriculum, making it hard for a shy child to make friends. Thoughtful and imaginative, Ben found no outlet for his intellectual or imaginative energies in school, and the rigidity of the scheduling — mixed with the need for quiet in large groups — meant there were few opportunities for the kind of spontaneous enjoyment which leads to friendship.

Ben's father grew lonely for the ordinary give-and-take of family life, which he missed because of his long commute. His mother missed his father and longed for some close friendships. The salary which had looked so big on paper didn't stretch very far in this part of the country. His parents started to quarrel. Ben tried to stop them, but when he found he couldn't make a difference, he just got quiet. Disappointment smoldered in each of them. Then, in response to two events, it ignited.

First, creeping suburban sprawl was crowding herds of raccoons out of their previous habitat and into Ben's family's neighborhood. At first, the animals seemed entertaining, but then they became real nuisances and finally dangerous, as rabies spread among them. Ben's little dog was bitten by one and had to be put down.

Ben was devastated and then furious. He was angry at his parents for having moved. He was angry along with them for the family's shared unhappiness. And, he was angry on their behalf. He wanted to protect them, and at the same time he wanted to punish them. These swirling, conflicting emotions scorched his heart. Not even realizing what he was doing, he took their wedding picture and smashed the glass. Appalled at himself, he tried to hide it. When hiding didn't work, sparks flew.

The second event was the arrival of a van used for dealing drugs. The day after the dog's death, gun shots broke out at the van.

Angry, frightened, their dreams in ashes, danger escalating around them, Ben's parents decided to pack up and go back where they had come from. A pay cut seemed worth it. Quality of life won out. They lost some money, they lost some job security, they lost a window on vastness and some false pride, but they opened the way for new growth on old ground.

Fire balls, their origins various but their destructive power consistent, consume themselves as well as whatever lies in their path. When anger swells to this dimension, the person — himself or herself — is swallowed in its violence. Consistent frustration, such as we saw with Floyd, can spawn a fireball. A combination of high standards and low self-esteem can ignite into a fireball. The straw that breaks the camel's back can be the match of conflagration. When all these pressures unite, a fireball is inevitable — sometimes threatening life, sometimes destroying it.

Lewis is in his early twenties now and well on his way to a productive, deeply satisfying career, but not without an attempt at suicide that resulted in hospitalization.

As a young child, Lewis was sensitive, creative, readily involved in stories and arts and crafts projects, and obviously intelligent, although he was neither macho nor physically robust. In his pre-school years, he had a series of recurrent middle-ear infections, which resulted in undetected, fluctuating hearing loss on both the left and right sides.

As is often true with children whose hearing is depressed, Lewis had a hard time learning to read, write, and spell, which frustrated him because he had always been so enthusiastic about books and stories. As he began to lose his confidence, his reading slipped farther behind until he was in the lowest reading group. At the same time, he had a hard time establishing his place with the other boys in his class, since he avoided the rough and tumble of contact sports.

In second grade, his ear infections returned, accompanied again by undetected hearing loss. One day, his teacher flew into a rage at him because he failed to follow a set of directions. She took him into the hall and made him stand in his locker, facing the wall, for an entire morning. He was, of course, frightened and humiliated, but also too pliant to recognize that he deserved to be angry. After that episode, he was afraid to go to school, and every day was a battle.

By sixth grade, although his intelligence was obvious to anyone who spent time with him, he was still a weak reader, seemed reluctant to tap his intellectual power, didn't speak out in class discussions, and was always the last boy chosen for athletic teams.

He became the class goat, and as his classmates proceeded into pre-adolescence, they dreamed up increasingly cruel ways of torturing and humiliating him.

Lewis didn't share his fear and sadness with his parents. His father was a very successful fellow, who only wanted to hear about strengths and triumphs. His mother was a gentle soul, rather ineffective and inclined to worry. There didn't seem to be much point in unburdening himself to them or seeking their advice.

During this time, though, he had a secret source of solace. He invented a cast of characters and created a mythical kingdom for them, including territories, dwellings, adversaries, and secret powers. Then, he wrote and illustrated their adventures, fashioned small action figures representing them, and, when things got rough in the real world, he would retreat to his fantasy realm.

At the end of eighth grade, his father decided that Lewis should be sent to boarding school. "It will make a man of him. No more dreaming around in his room. Boarding school will have the boy out there doing things, playing sports."

Lewis went, reluctantly, but with a sliver of optimism. Maybe things would be different in a new place. Unfortunately, though, as is usually the case, he brought his problems along with him, and soon was again the class goat. The difference was that in boarding school he had to be with his classmates 24 hours a day, instead of only 7 or 8.

He signed up for a slot on the school newspaper, had some legitimate success, and was starting to make a few friends, but he was removed from the position because of low grades in History and Mechanics of English. The school provided some tutoring which seemed effective, and he continued writing his adventure series, albeit in the deepest secrecy. The following year, he signed up for the newspaper again, and also for the class play. One evening when he was at rehearsal, some kids went into his room and found his collection of action figures, illustrations, and stories. They scribbled over everything with a black, indelible marker. They dumped the whole defaced collection into a cardboard carton. They labeled it "Our Boy's Toys," and put it in the front hall of the dormitory.

When Lewis came back from rehearsal, they were waiting to see his reaction. Unsuspecting, he came in the door. He saw the box, and, with mounting dread, started pawing through it, even slipping into some of the voices he had invented for his characters, as panic, anger, and embarrassment engulfed him. When he looked up and saw the other kids sitting on the stairs laughing, he burst into tears. That only made the other kids laugh harder and louder. Lewis picked up the box, fled to his room, locked his door, took his Swiss Army knife and slit his wrists.

Fortunately, one of the perpetrators felt remorseful and frightened by Lewis's reaction. The boy went to the housemaster, who reached Lewis in time to get him to the hospital.

In the aftermath, Lewis and his parents received extensive counseling, he took a solid course of tutoring to learn to compensate for the undiagnosed dyslexia which, along with the undetected hearing loss, had been pulling him down academically, and found courses in creative writing and in drawing at the nearby community college. The boy bloomed. At this writing, several years later, Lewis is the recipient of a prestigious journalism award for a newspaper series he wrote on the topic of child abuse, and has a contract with a New York publisher for a series of four books drawn from his early fiction.

The build-up to Lewis's fireball is easy to see in hindsight. With foresight, he might not have had to come so close to metaphoric and actual death.

Although this book is not about deep pathology, this is the moment to say, unequivocally, that whenever a parent, teacher, or other adult hears a child mention suicide or make such statements such as "Life's not worth living," "I'd be better off dead," "If I were dead I wouldn't have to feel this bad," it is imperative to seek psychiatric help IMMEDIATELY. This is no time to hold back from fear of being an alarmist or a cry-wolf. Such statements, whether made overtly or simply insinuated, deserve immediate attention.

Our final fire metaphor is benevolent: a camp fire or fire contained in a fireplace. Ignited on purpose, it is a rallying point for shared safety and warmth. The same is true of anger.

Focused anger against injustice or impropriety is a blazing force. When a neighborhood house was seriously damaged in a racist incident, the children and parents who lived nearby rallied around. They collected clothing, toys, and bikes for the target kids; food and furnishings for everyone; and organized a campfire, Hootenanny, car wash, and bake sale, with all proceeds to go for the repair of damages. A group of parents volunteered their time on weekends, rebuilding and refurbishing. Finally, the work was done. What had been destroyed by a dreadful kind of anger had been restored by common outrage converted to common purpose.

The kinds of fires we have looked at in this chapter illustrate both potentials of heat: productive and destructive. To respond constructively, we now need to consider the distinctions among:

legitimate anger
habitual anger
inappropriate anger
repressed anger

Tips for managing and channeling anger are in the next section of this chapter.

Legitimate Anger   A child whose domestic security is shattered by divorce, death, the arrival of a sibling, or being moved away from familiar surroundings has a right to feel angry. Something important has been taken away, and anger is a wholly legitimate response to loss.

A child who is humiliated, undervalued, or treated with sarcasm has a right to be angry.

A child whose treasures are disturbed, broken, or mocked has a right to anger.

A child who suffers consistent frustration is entitled to the self-defence of anger.

A child who cannot do with effort what others do with ease — be it learning, scoring a soccer goal, or pleasing a parent — has reason to be angry.

A child consistently denied the power to make decisions (at an age-appropriate level) has a right to feel angry. To always be an object of other people's planning, instead of an agent of one's own destiny, is dehumanizing.

A child may use anger as a way of trying to make order out of chaos, seeking to impose control on external situations or raging internal impulses.

A child who lacks needed food, shelter, and safety has every reason to be angry.

Obviously, I intend the above categories to cover any and all forms of abuse.

Habitual Anger

Habitual anger may be legitimate — springing from any of the causes just described — just as legitimate anger becomes habitual when conditions are consistently unfair or oppressive. These are easy to understand and anticipate. But, sometimes a kid transfers a legitimately angry response from one situation to the other experiences life offers. People comment, "That kid has a chip on his (her) shoulder."

Habits are hard to break. Anger is a bad habit, and, because it drives people away, may increase the angry person's isolation — which, in turn, may be a fundamental part of the anger. We will see more of this in the section, One Child's Story.

In addition (or in parallel) to the sources of legitimate anger listed above, the habit of anger may be born of:

being misunderstood

feeling undervalued

struggling with undiagnosed learning problems

trying to control Attention Deficit Disorder (ADD)

having the carrot always moved just out of reach

parental inconsistency

a teacher's inconsistency

unfair treatment

low self-esteem

having to be always on guard (the best defense is a good offense)

lack of success (real or perceived)

pessimistic explanatory style: "I always mess up" (see pages 69 and 70)

Inappropriate Anger In contrast to legitimate or habitual anger, it can be very hard to ferret out the sources of inappropriate anger. When minor irritations cause major firestorms, we need to ask whether we are seeing embers of unrighted wrongs, the eruption of constantly roiling molten rock, or spontaneous combustion.

We know that kids who have been unwilling spectators (or objects of) abuse often react consistently with major intensity to minor problems. This is an important diagnostic signal.

Anger is inappropriate:

when it is misdirected

when kids get angry at themselves for things that are not their fault

when kids get angry at others for situations they have caused themselves

We should seek professional guidance when there is:

disproportion between the magnitude of an event and the angry response

frequent loss of control

when the angry child doesn't have (or can't) find a happy self to return to

any mention of self-destruction or not wanting to continue living

Repressed *Anger*	Returning to our opening question about the relationship between anger and danger, unchanneled, repressed anger threatens both the child who bears it and those in the child's circle.

We know from Erik Erikson that habitual feelings of shame and guilt predispose children to trouble resolving the inevitable conflicts of growth. Depression is one form (and one consequence) of anger turned inward. We know, too, that the incidence of clinical depression in school-age children is seriously underestimated.

We saw on page 71 how depression may be camouflaged by boisterous, unfocused behaviors. In addition, we need to notice such indicators as sadness, listlessness, expressions of ineffectuality, explanatory style, and the words which say — or the behaviors which imply — "I'm no good..."

when the kid's basic stance is apologetic

I once evaluated a fourth grade boy who, though obviously bright, was not delivering the academic goods. When I dropped the cards we were going to use in one sub-test, HE flinched and said, "Oh, I'm sorry. My fault." He had been nowhere near the cards, it was all my fault, and furthermore, since they were easy to pick up, it was really a nonevent. On further, deeper diagnosis, he proved to be clinically depressed.

when kids don't stick up for themselves

If a little sister demolishes a Lego creation, a classmate breaks an art project, or a peer grabs a toy, anger is a natural response. "Mr. Nice Guy" and "Ms. Make Nice" may be making peace at their own expense. If they would feel guilty speaking on their own behalf, they need to learn how to channel and express their grievances.

when children lose a parent to separation, divorce, or death and act as if nothing had happened

"He's taken right up where his father left off," "She's taking care of the little ones as if she were their mother," and "A perfect little adult" all suggest unexpressed anger, which is like fire in a peat bog. The child needs to learn how to bring it to the surface. Energies required in the denial of grief steal from the supply the child needs for learning.

when children feel guilty about feeling angry

"They told me not to yell at my brother, but I did anyway, and now they're getting separated" is how many kids feel about the breakup of their parents' marriage. They say, in effect, "My anger is so dangerous, it blew the family apart. I better not ever have any more of it." "Anger is danger. Look what it's done already. I'd better stifle it." Or, a child may feel guilty about his own anger in response to a situation: "I hate my Dad for leaving."

Think of the effort needed to shove a jack-in-the-box back into captivity, or the concentration needed to keep it there while getting the lid down and secured. This is the kind of attention required — in a sustained way — to keep anger locked away. Constant vigilance and alertness to any threat of escape or explosion absorb the child's emotional and intellectual attentions, leaving little for learning.

when children or grown-ups don't know they are furious

"I just love this baby," says the 3-year-old sibling, with one hand squeezing the infant's foot and with the other giving long, deep pokes in its stomach.

An acquaintance I meet out walking reminds me of one of those toys whose rotating layers make different combinations of hair, forehead, eyes, nose, and mouth. This man's mouth smiles when he says, "Hello," but his eyes smoulder with irritation and impatience. He yanks his dog leash and huffs away, probably thinking himself a charming fellow.

When I asked Everett to bring his favorite stuffed animal to school, his eyes brimmed with tears, he smiled, and said, "My mother said third graders are too big to play with stuffed toys, so she gave all mine away one day when I was in school." He smiled more broadly. A few days later, I said, "Ev, what do you do when you feel sad?" He answered, "I smile." "What do you do when you are angry?" I asked. "I grin."

We know from previous examples that children pay a high price in lost learning for their attempts to deny their anger.

aiming low so failure is impossible

"I like to lose," said the 10-year-old boy playing cards.

Ten Tips for Moms, Dads, Nannies, Grannies, Grandfathers, Teachers, and Other Concerned Adults

1. "Letting It All Hang Out" and "Prompting the Primal Scream" were hot stuff in psychobabble a few years ago. But, current thinking puts greater stock in channeling anger, while also keeping it from going underground to cause subterranean pain and destruction. We need to help kids convert destructive anger to constructive pursuits, acknowledging its presence while keeping it within bounds. The goal is to change the child's stance from victim of one's own anger to acknowledger, channeler, and user.

Language is one of the most effective tools. Even the little child can learn "use words," "tell me how you feel," "you can explain. I'll listen."

Counting to ten or reciting the alphabet, the Gettysburg Address, or a selection of poetry inserts time and a linguistic buffer between anger and acting out.

2. Children need appropriate areas of control. Adults can provide this without abdicating authority. Example:"Do you want to clean up the toys before supper or after?" or "Which of these three shirts would you like to wear tomorrow?"

3. It's Not a Perfect World...Yet. Using alphabetical order, help the child (ren) chart anger-sparkers from A-Z. Then choose one, make up a story based on such a situation, and devise an ending which will put things to rights.

4. Time heals. Working with children and anger, adults must first be sure kids understand the concept of time, can postpone gratification, have a logical sense of anticipation, and can organize their experiences and emotions in temporal sequence. Then, together, adults and children need:

time to listen
time to intuit
time to share

Here are a few examples:

Many children feel, rightly or wrongly, that adults don't listen to them. In response, one mother said, "We eat salad every night. The ten minutes while I am chopping carrots and slicing mushrooms belong entirely to you. I won't answer the phone or talk to anyone else."

Parents and teachers almost always know what's going on inside their kids, but sometimes they need to communicate this intuition. "It seems to me you've been disappointed about quite a few things this week. If you want to tell me about them, I'll be glad to listen."

A father of a consistently angry 8-year-old son, the middle child in the family, said, "Tuesdays are going to be Henry's and my day to have a breakfast date." They went to IHOP (International House of Pancakes), which only took a little time and a little money, and gave the child a special, private time.

5. Flip-Flop involves inventing two stories. The first will tell something you did that made someone else angry, and how you might make restitution. The second will be something someone did to you that made you angry, and how restitution was made. Children need to be creatively involved in thinking about making others angry, as well as being angry themselves. A collection of home-made or store-bought puppets comes in handy.

6. Physical outlets. A punching bag, a run around the house, one hundred jumps on a jump rope, a set of push-ups or sit-ups can provide a safe physical outlet for emotional fire. Karate teaches how to develop and maintain control in the presence of excitement, as does athletic practice of other kinds.

7. Time out. This non-judgmental technique for helping a kid cool down works by physically separating the child from the situation for a specified amount of time, making the point that the behavior is not permissible, but without saying that the child is a bad person.

8. Children need chances to make restitution for their harmful, hurtful acts. A child who writes a bad word on a wall in school can stay late to scrub the wall, or give it a fresh coat of paint, perhaps even having to buy the paint from his or her allowance or earnings.

9. Each child needs a place at home that can be a sanctuary. For children who don't have their own rooms, the place can be his or her bed, or a chair in the bedroom or the family room. The point is to have a refuge. The same principle holds true in school, and can take the form of a solo project which is equally sacrosanct. A folder of math puzzles, poetry, or a journal could each offer a "place" to go for a little time out or an intellectual breather.

10. The challenge of serious intellectual work can convert anger to purpose. Anger is the initial fuel; the rocket is the product.

Six Specific Activities For Teachers

These suggestions dovetail with the six priorities outlined in Chapter One.

1. *By Heart.* Children who know a speech or a play or poetry by heart have an internal resource of potential calm — a sort of "count to ten" magnified. Let each child in the class choose something to memorize, and then provide a showcase for showmanship. Perhaps Fridays after recess could be "Show Time."

2. *Keeper of the Feely Bag.* Most teachers are familiar with the generic Feely Bag, a sack or paper bag into which are put various familiar objects. Two children are chosen to be "Its" and leave the room. The others decide which object to put in this day's Feely Bag. When summoned, the "Its" return; one is the describer, the other the guesser. The describer is blindfolded or trusted not to look, puts one hand in the Feely Bag, and describes the object by properties: "It is hard, rectangular, and has two holes with cogs." The guesser tries to figure out what the object is: "Is it a cassette?"

The keeper of the Feely Bag becomes a custodian of fun and suspense, having appropriate doses of power, autonomy, preparation, and control, and a chance to play a benevolent role. This change in persona is often very important for habitually angry kids.

3. *Pick a Field From A-V.* (See Chapter Three for A-V.) Pick one field of endeavor from this list. Research and chart five things a person in that field must know or be able to do, five sources of training and information, five common obstacles/problems in the field, and five good ways to cope with those difficulties. Let each child choose one, and then plan a time when they can share their ideas with their class or even with other classes. The child who charts obstacles and difficulties begins to feel mastery over them. Feelings of autonomy often pull the fangs of anger.

4. *Glorious Villains.* Ask each child in the class to choose a favorite villain from a story they have heard, read, or written (not seen on TV or in the movies). Ask them to choose how to describe that villain to the other members of the class, so they will discover why it is a villain; how the villain looks, sounds, and smells; what bad things the villain does; and what force can keep the villain in place.

5. *Twenty Ways.* Ask each child to develop a list or chart of twenty ways for teachers and students themselves to measure academic progress. Of course, one option can be testing, through quizzes or exams. But, can each child think up 19 additional ways?

One sixth grader, whose aggressive behavior seemed to spring from always being told what to do, seized this opportunity. In the first week, he came up with ten: tape recorder descriptions, portfolios, exhibitions, putting on a play, writing a newspaper, making a diorama, acting out a skit, writing "Shrink Lits," cooperative learning group performances, kids writing the test questions. Now in the second week, he is still enjoying planning from the measurer's seat instead of always being the one who gets measured.

Led by such researchers and practitioners as Theodore Sizer and Howard Gardner, some of the most exciting educational leaders are focusing on alternative measures of mastery, and the role of teacher as coach vs. the role of teacher as controller.

6. *Ringer.* Give each child a notebook ring and a set of index cards. Ask them to write one negative emotion on each card, then choose one and write a story incorporating it, or develop a skit with some others to act out the emotion — showing body English, causes, and cures.

Legitimizing negative emotions makes anger a permissible piece of the human emotional landscape. Solving problems through story or drama shows children that they can make good things happen, and that temporarily difficult situations can turn out well. Optimism feeds enthusiasm. Enthusiasm feeds learning.

ONE CHILD'S STORY
"Is This Really Me?"

"I hate you! You shouldn't have done that. I can't trust anyone!" Sarah slammed the door to her room, leaving her parents standing frightened and ashamed, not knowing what to do next.

"I know diaries are private," her mother said to Sarah's father. "But, I've been uneasy about her lately, and when she left the diary on the kitchen counter, I just picked it up out of curiosity. Then, when I saw the part about death being a form of peace and how much being alive hurts, I panicked. That's when I called you, and she overheard me on the phone."

From behind Sarah's slammed, now locked, door came the sounds of rage and despair. "I hate those kids in school. I hate you. I hate myself. I hate being alive."

Her mother and father went to her door. "Sarah, we love you."

"No, you don't. You move me around like a piece on a checkers board. Your new job always matters more than I do."

"Please come out, honey, so we can talk."

"Why should I? You're always too busy for me. You always have lots to do, and you know lots of people, and you can talk to each other. I don't have anybody. I don't have any friends, and I don't even want to because I hate all those dumb kids in school."

"You won't come out?"

"No. Leave me alone."

Sarah's mother stayed by the locked door, while her father went to the phone to call his sister, a psychologist who — although she lives far away — has always had a special fondness for Sarah. He recounted the episode and said, "Margo, we're very frightened. We don't know what to do. We feel guilty about having read the diary, but at least it alerted us to the depths of Sarah's unhappiness."

"I wouldn't feel so guilty about that," Margo responded. "If she left the diary on the counter in the kitchen, she was asking for it to be read. I think she put it there with the unconscious intention of your reading it and hearing her cry for help."

"What can we do? How can we get her to come out of her room?" Paul asked.

"That's the easy part," Margo answered. "We need to figure out how she got into this state in the first place. Then, we'll figure out how to get her out of it. Does she still read all the time? The last time I visited, she never took her nose out of her book. I know you were both so proud that she's a good student, but I wondered if she mightn't be using all that reading as an escape. Has anybody from this new school called her for a play date, or to go out for a pizza?"

"No, I don't think so. I'd have to check to be sure, but she says she doesn't like any of the other kids."

"That's probably her way of telling you she doesn't like herself, don't you think, and also a face-saving way to tell you (and herself) that they don't like her," Margo said. "If you don't like yourself, you only have anger and unpleasantness to offer out for friendship, and they don't usually attract many takers. Is she in touch with any of the kids from the school she was in last year or the year before? Any phone calls or letters? Do they ever see each other over the summer or anything?"

"No. I guess when we move we don't make much of an effort to stay in touch. We move so often. You know, rolling stones gather no moss. Isn't that how the saying goes?"

"But, the child may be dying to gather some moss," Margo suggested. "Is this friendlessness new to this move, or has it been a pattern all along?"

"I'm not sure. I guess I never paid much attention. I mean she seemed OK, and we brought her up the way we did the others. They're OK, so I guess I just assumed she is, too. She always gets good grades. What are you thinking?"

"Lots of times big people think that because children come in small sizes, they can't have giant feelings. That's not true. Sometimes, kids are scared of powerful feelings like anger, so they try to ignore them, or pretend them away, or forget them by trying to lose themselves in story books. But, feelings insist on coming out. Sometimes, kids who are angry underneath act unpleasant to other kids without realizing it. Their voices, their body English, their choice of words are hostile, but they don't see these things in themselves, so they don't understand why other kids don't like them."

"But, what does she have to be so angry about? She has every piece of equipment you can name, and actually she gets anything she asks for. We love her."

"Yes. You and her mother love her very much. I know that. But, providing her with material things isn't the point. And, she may not realize how deeply you care about her. Also, you may not have been showing her that side of yourselves. She is old enough to need friends — the warmth of connection." Margo waited for her brother's reply.

"Well, be that as it may, we haven't done anything wrong intentionally, and it scares me to have her even thinking about death. She's just a kid," Paul said. "And, I want her to come out of that room."

"The fact that she has erupted this way may mean her energy is spent, and she's not thinking about hurting herself. But, we must never make that assumption. She needs to be seen by a psychiatrist or a psychologist immediately to be sure. You can call your own doctor, or your local hospital, or you can look in the yellow pages under Social and Human Services. You'll find a slew of resources.

"Then, I think you should go to her door and say in a firm but loving voice, 'Sarah, your mother and I can't let you go on hurting like this. We have some ways to help, and we want to listen to everything you want to say. We're going to go into the den, and we need to have you come there with us. We can help stop the hurt, but you need to work on this with us.'

"Go in the den and wait. I bet she'll be there within half an hour. When she gets there, hold her tight, tell her you love her and that you're going to go with her for a checkup with a doctor, who will make some suggestions. Call me back."

Paul went to Sarah's door and, holding his wife's hand, said what Margo had told him to say. Then, they walked into the den and waited.

In about ten minutes, they heard the refrigerator door open and close. "I needed some milk," Sarah said tentatively. Her father and mother went to the kitchen, held her tight, and said, "It's time to talk."

On examination, Sarah proved not to be suicidal, but to be angry, sad, and lonely. These emotions frequently go together, reinforce one another's negative powers, and need to be addressed. Anger turned outward makes conflict. Anger turned inward feeds depression and thoughts of self-harm or destruction. Anger repressed escapes anyway.

Sarah and her parents needed help in recognizing the anger she felt at her frequent relocations, and her sense of abandonment when she and her family would arrive in a new community together, but her parents would go about their new lives, leaving her to try to make friends on her own.

Sarah is the youngest child in her family, separated in age from her nearest sibling by fifteen years. Because her father is an engineer who changed business location frequently, Sarah had lived in eight states before she turned 10. After arriving in a new community, she would just begin to feel settled, maybe have the tenuous beginnings of a friendship, just be learning the local terminology (hoagie, grinder, submarine, Dagwood), and sensing her way around the town or village, when WHAM, they would move again.

With these frequent dislocations grew a sense of urgency about being accepted and making friends. In her eagerness, she would come on too strong, and the other children would pull away. Sensing this, she would try harder to get their attention or their favor, and a familiar negative spiral would begin. She would escape by losing herself in books. Reading was her refuge, but it didn't address the problems.

This current crisis led Sarah and her parents to some solutions:

First, they had a short series of counseling sessions to air some past hurts and begin some new practices.

Second, as a family, they joined an "Orienteering Club," which offered Saturday and Sunday explorations. They met other people — young and old — in a setting of shared activity. This took the pressure off Sarah's immature and unsuccessful social skills, letting her find companionship through common adventure instead. Three weeks into the program, Paul called his sister and said, "Well, we're all learning to read compasses and maps, but what we're really finding is ourselves and one another."

Also, Sarah joined the basketball team at school. This fast-moving sport is a splendid outlet for aggressive energies, and Sarah is well-coordinated. Other kids began to see her in a positive light. Her parents had a long talk with the coach, during which they told him Sarah's recent history, and asked him to help her with social issues when he could. He taught Sarah to play as a teammate instead of as a solo practitioner, and slipped her some phrases to use in praising another kid's shot or just entering the locker room.

At Halloween, a local group got together to create parties for people in the convalescent hospital at the retirement community, which happened to be near Sarah's house. Several of the youngsters — Sarah among them — enjoyed the older people's companionship and their obvious delight in being with younger people. They agreed to meet once a month, and to make up a reason for a party if a holiday wasn't coming up. In these meetings, Sarah heard about a great variety of places people had lived, moves they had made, old friends, memories, and the importance of new friends. She began to see her own experiences in a new light.

Last year, through an announcement in the local paper, Sarah's mother found something called "The OKCamp Experience." Sarah gathered up her courage and enrolled for a week away from home. These are her words about the experience:

"Imagine living in an environment where everybody liked you and you liked them, not just as acquaintances but as friends...an environment where people could relate to and trust each other with deep confidences. This happened at The OKCamp Experience. If bad vibrations developed among people, those in control confronted the situation openly, so that it disappeared and everyone was able to be as open with others as they had been before. Thus, an environment — unimaginable in the real school world I had known — was created. How was this possible?

"The campers were divided into groups of eight individuals, who were to be as open as possible with one another. To begin with, they were to express positive feelings about themselves and each other. The first goal was to give and receive compliments without being bashful. Once people felt good about themselves, it was easier to share feelings and let old, hard, hurting emotions out. Once the pain was not just in oneself, it became easier to be positive, to believe that one could do anything one put a mind to. The first step was to be kind to people, to learn to trust them, and, most importantly, to listen to what they had to say and to see their hearts. Sharing sessions enabled all members to let go of closely held secrets about themselves and their families. These meetings were often very emotional, and the members learned to cry for themselves and others without embarrassment.

"The mutual trust that slowly developed was put to the test with the ropes course, which involved putting one's life in others' hands. Each member of the group climbed to the top of a sixty-foot pole, with safety lines in the hands of others whom they trusted. Then, they would jump out into the air trying to reach a moving bar — a symbol of their life's goals.

"Once these initial relationships were formed, the members of the group began to take real responsibility for their actions. They realized they always had choices, so that they could stop and think before they acted. They could be honest, and therefore trust themselves and others more. The Golden Rule was made reality in this environment, for the more trust one puts into a relationship, the more meaningful it becomes and the better people feel about themselves. Some truths which became self-evident were:

'Failure is never final.'

'I have the power to make my dreams happen.'

'The ability to give the best of oneself and to show one's appreciation of life is the most important. In the process of ameliorating oneself, one must circumsect* and always be tenacious.'

"The OKCamp Experience was a sheltered environment, where everyone could succeed. Although the real world is very different, the courage each member of the group gained made it possible to confront the outside world with confidence and friendliness."

Handing it in, she wrote at the bottom of the last page, "Is this really me? Part of me doesn't dare believe it, but another part wants to shout it out, 'I love being alive!'"

*Sarah's word

Chapter FIVE

CHILDREN ON PEDESTALS

The Perils of Worship,
The Power of Love

All parents have dreams for their children, and often make willing and appropriate sacrifices to bring those dreams to life. But, some get carried away, stepping over the line dividing hope and encouragement from worship. This chapter explores that boundary, and the emotional and academic consequences of — intentionally or unintentionally — standing on the dangerous side of the divider.

In a kind of emotional Midas-ism, children on pedestals are deprived of their own humanity. Their personal needs, feelings, stirrings, ideas, and goals are subsumed in the plans, priorities, and passions of their worshippers.

Some worshipping parents simply extend their own ambitions through a child. Ten-year-old Ian said, "I feel like toothpaste being squeezed through somebody else's tube."

Other worshipping parents abdicate their own authority, give the child his or her head, take a secondary position, and put their offspring on a pedestal for the rest of the world to see and admire.

That these behaviors are more misguided than malevolent doesn't diminish their harmful effect. Worshipped children lose touch with those realities of cause and effect, which underlie solid relationships as well as genuine academic achievement. They are separated from humanity rather than joined to it. And, underneath the temporary warmth from the spotlight, they chill to the loneliness of isolation.

The old-fashioned word is "spoiled." But, while the children in this chapter are often spoiled, worshipped means something deeper and darker. The perils and deprivations of worship cross all socioeconomic lines.

Among the wealthy who fall into these behaviors, the worshipped child's whims are gratified immediately, and if school problems arise, "We'll HIRE a teacher, or give a gymnasium. You'll be the top (or get the prize)...you'll see." Or, "Rules are for others." This separates the child from personal problems or achievements, permitting escape from the former while diminishing the latter.

In the middle economic range, we may hear parents say, "I don't want my kid to have to struggle the way I did. He (she) will have everything I (we) didn't have. I'll find a way." Often, these parents make serious sacrifices to buy the type of schooling — or number and assortment of lessons — designed to place the child in the academic or social diadem. If the adult's plans match the child's own nature and dreams, well and good. But, if the goals are superimposed on a reluctant participant, emotional and intellectual energies will travel elsewhere.

Parents with limited economic resources may select one child: "Davey's the one we'll send to college." But, as we know from folklore, family living, and *Joseph and the Amazing Technicolor Dreamcoat*, "first-among-equals" status promotes jealousy, and may raise discomfort or guilt inside the chosen child. Ironically, in exchange for receiving adulation and material gain, the worshipped child is denied the foibles, successes, failures, and humor of being human.

The issues involved in daily living can blur the line separating worship and love. Because appropriate love is the greatest gift any child can receive, and because worship actually deprives the child of genuine love, parents and teachers need to explore this question carefully.

Parents may discover new aspects in their own behaviors, their children's patterns, or the stances of their children's friends. We know from experience — and will see in the next chapter — friendships are powerful influences. The more parents understand what is going on in the child's circle, the more they can encourage the wholesome and counteract the undesirable.

Teachers deal frequently with the issues worshipped children raise, and manage them more effectively when they understand the whole pattern of deluge and deprivation.

In our exploration, we need to ask four questions:

1. How and why does normal parental pride and love shift into worship?

2. Where is the boundary between the appropriate and the destructive?

3. What are the emotional and educational results of being worshipped?

4. Can we break maladaptive patterns without breaking spirit?

1. How and why does normal parental pride and love shift into worship?

Here are eleven examples. Of course, not all parents or children who fit these outward circumstances fall into the worshipped child trap, but most who are in the trap fit one or more of these situations.

The Long-Awaited Baby When the mother or father (or both) reach a certain rung on the career ladder — with money in the bank, a title on the door and an interesting or high-level job to return to after maternity leave, (and with the biological clock ticking) — the happy couple jettisons the birth control and waits for nature to take its course. Wait they often do.

Tears, tests, and medications become part of the process. Then, whether the awaited miracle happens spontaneously or via a petri dish, conception brings joy, plans, and vows of perfect parenthood. Adoption works the same way. New life brings awe and reverence, as it always should; but this awe and reverence, growing as rapidly as the child, shifts into Deification of Superbaby. In school, Superbaby usually has trouble becoming a member of the group, and Superbaby's parents have trouble acknowledging problems or receiving suggestions.

In contrast, my young friend, Babs, the mother of twins now 4-years-old, says, "Charlie and I had waited SO long. I knew what a great father he'd be, and I've wanted to be a mother ever since I pulled my Teddy bear around in my wagon. I think having twins saved everybody. We were so tired that the whole first year was just a blur. Someone always needed something. We didn't have time for that worship stuff. Love...? Plenty. But worship? We were both too busy figuring out how to get some sleep!"

Trophy Baby The traditional cast of characters in this drama includes an older father married to a much younger wife, their trophy baby, and, in the background, his previous wife (or wives), and his first and perhaps second flotilla of children.

In the classic story line, the father spends his early years scrambling up the corporate ladder, missing class plays and soccer games. His first marriage disintegrates, the children have subsequent trouble with schoolwork, and often with alcohol and other drugs. Divorced, the father pays over the agreed upon monies to his former spouse(s), and resents being genetically, emotionally, and financially shackled to his disappointing, unsuccessful offspring.

Enter Spring, in the form of the Trophy Wife. She longs for a baby. He, by now successful enough to drive a swell car and skip out on a couple of meetings in favor of a class play or soccer game, decides to grant her wish, display his own virility, and give parenthood another whirl.

He determines not to make any of the old mistakes. Time, attention, and heart's desires will surround his new child. His young wife, inexperienced in some ways but intuitively attuned to inter-wife competition, assures herself that the combination of her maternal instincts, his support, and the child's own perfection will make this baby better than any from the previous lot(s). Enter Trophy Baby. Bring on the pedestal.

Later, the child's discovery of another world called school, with its expectations and requirements, creates internal shock waves which jostle emotional equilibrium and the child's enthusiasm for doing the temporarily hard work which leads to long-term learning.

"It's A Girl!" or "It' A Boy!" When one sex has dominated a family, and a child of the other sex arrives, it's a cause for celebration, often mixed with terror and awe. These emotions may be set to refrains of "No hand-me-downs for Amelia" or "Boys Will Be Boys."

When, after four boys, a daughter was born to a family we know well, their friends hung a pink banner in the post office. Every one in the small town rejoiced, understanding the signal. That child was dressed in pink from head to toe, her father bought a new baby carriage, new high chair, and new crib. "She deserves a fresh start. No hand-me-downs for Amelia."

Another family we also know well had a son when their daughters were nearly in high school. They had been an orderly group — the girls were responsible, courteous, and well-liked by both peers and family friends. But, with the male child's arrival, the firm, fair discipline the parents had exercised with their daughters evaporated. The little prince would throw his food on the floor if it didn't please him. His mother would mop up and then fetch what he was bellowing for. He kicked soccer balls in the living room, knocked over people's drinks, interrupted, jumped fully-shod on the furniture, and was in all ways the model of a Goop. Others winced, but his parents would smile through their fatigued forbearance, roll their eyes, and say, "Boys will be boys."

When parental vision is clouded by assumptions of perfection, children cannot find a realistic context for themselves. This lack distorts their ability to function in school, as well as in the big, wide world.

The Gifted Child

Children with exceptional intelligence or talents are often put on pedestals by their parents. Then, because they have children's natural inclinations to test authority, and because they are highly intelligent and plan their campaigns skillfully, they press harder than others for later bed times, freedom from such family chores as taking out the trash, and general permissions of one sort or another. At the first hint of parental resistance, they threaten — or throw — temper tantrums. Intimidated parents give these tiny tyrants their heads.

In the long run, this is a cruel cop-out. While all children like — and need — to test the limits, they also need the psychological safety of being cared for by people who are willing to be in charge. When children can bamboozle their caretakers, they lose their protectors. This is terrifying.

Adolescents press at the limits as hard as they can, often begging — under their bluster — for a firm, kind "No." Parents who are overawed by a child's talent for music, who are outstripped by a progeny's knowledge of math, or are flattened by youthful verbal skills, may lose sight of the child's need for parents to be kindly but firmly in control. I call this the "Prayer of the Adolescent:"

I'll fight my parents
Through thick and thin
And please, dear God,
Don't let me win.

Physically Beautiful Children

Who knows whether Elizabeth Taylor would have had a better life, given lower wattage in her violet eyes. Physical beauty compels attention and makes people want to touch.

All little children are beautiful, but some are more so. I think particularly of one girl and one boy.

Bess has a cap of copper curls, and her skin is fair without a freckle in sight. Her eyes are a deep, cornflower blue with thick dark lashes, and she has a small cleft in her chin.

She moves with a dancer's rhythmic grace, and because movement gives her pleasure, she is frequently in motion. Her diving is a fusion of precision and beauty. Watching her prepare to serve a tennis ball is to see a quiet centering, an inward gathering of strength and rhythm, a walling off of distraction. When she tosses the ball, raises her racket, and connects, the ball flies where it is aimed, and she moves into position for its return. Skating, skiing, and other winter sports bring high color to her cheeks, and the combination of grace, hair, cheeks, eyes, and dimple leave people simply staring.

Like many who love athletics and movement in space, Bess prefers actions to words. She was a late talker in childhood, and is a reluctant conversationalist in school. Her physical beauty magnetizes people who, if polite, refrain from touching her physically, but touch her with their words instead. When she is slow to respond, she is correctly perceived as verbally awkward, or incorrectly thought to be haughty.

Her parents, awed by her beauty and physical skills, yet wanting her to be easier with words for academic as well as social reasons, registered her for some after-school activities which emphasized sharing through talking. Her participation was marginal at best, and a battle for control ensued which she, of course, won. You can't make another person talk. Oddly and sadly, her sustained victory in the silent war increased her parents' awe of her, and they moved her to an even higher pedestal.

In contrast, "Wiggles" makes the most of his looks. William Ruggles the 3rd — shortened to Wiggles — has blonde hair, hazel eyes, a thicket of long eyelashes, an athletic build, and a lop-sided smile that gives him an appealing air of vulnerability.

From earliest childhood, he was strikingly handsome, and, as early as age 2, he learned to have his own way, deflecting anger with his famous smile. He discovered, too, how to make the world dance for him by withholding that smile, and how to use physical magnetism to get out of trouble or into favor. In school, he used his smile with both peers and teachers. Now in eighth grade, he is discovering fuller power as he turns his charms to girls. Selfish, manipulative, and anything but the vulnerable, sweet fellow his smile implies, he's racking up the victories and getting away with murder.

My Son, the Doctor

Parental pride is a two-way force: parents applaud their progeny's achievements; children are proud to please their parents. But, sometimes pride in the work of a living human being shifts over to worship of the initials at the end of the person's name. M.D., Ph.D., or J.D. become equivalent to the "R" designating a king or queen.

My Son, the Doctor can do no wrong; it is others who are flawed. The script for this play is set early in the boy's childhood.

There may be trouble enough when the story unfolds according to plan. But, if My Son doesn't succeed, denial abounds, pressures increase, and anger seeps out sideways — directed at "the system" or "others" who have theoretically usurped power or overlooked talent.

Rob, short for Robinson F. Walters, Jr., was the heir apparent of a family highly placed in the American industrial hierarchy. His father, traditionally educated and now a powerful business man, married a woman he met in graduate school, when she was in the United States visiting a relative. The traditions of her European background dictated that a wife should stay at home, help her husband from the background, and raise the children. Rob was their first child, followed by two daughters — Elena and Christina.

From the very beginning, Rob was an average student. He was in the middle group for both math and reading, showed moderate athletic ability, and was reasonably well-liked. His father expected him to do better, his mother worried that she should be doing more about the boy, and the paternal grandparents offered to pay for a tutor and a private coach.

Patterns of average achievement continued through middle school, but whereas Rob had been a sunny child in his earlier years, the constant setting of unreachable goals eroded his self-concept. His smile faded. His temper grew short, and his general demeanor became a combination of sad and sour.

In conferences, Rob's father urged the boy's teachers to apply more pressure. To the outside world, his parents pretended the boy was "just too busy being a boy to concentrate on his schoolwork," while telling each other that "a turn-around is just around the corner."

With Elena and Christina doing beautifully at school, Rob's parents felt caught between accepting average standing and applying pressure to reach the top.

In tenth grade, Rob was given a major part in the class play. His father said, "I'll come see the play if Rob has all B's or higher on his report card. These are the years to focus on earning a high grade point average."

Two years later, Rob was not accepted at the Alma Mater in spite of his father's large donation to the Annual Fund. His father railed against "them;" his mother blamed herself for flawed nurturing. Rob, denied acceptance of himself and apologetic for who he was and would become, felt ashamed of his perfectly respectable scores and achievements.

Enrolled in a nearby college, he became involved with drugs. His parents bought his way out of trouble, but couldn't bring themselves to buy him therapy and treatment. To the world, they referred to "pranks" and "capers," and talked of where he would go to graduate school. In February of his senior year in college, Rob received a failing grade in history, jeopardizing his graduation. He took his own life.

My Daughter, the Deity (and her close relative, Deputy Princess)

Much psychiatry, psychology, and sociology have focused on mother-daughter relationships. In *Women and Their Fathers: The Sexual and Romantic Impact of the First Man in Your Life*, Victoria Secunda posits that many predominant emotional stances in growing and mature women are the fruit of encouragement and intimacy — or lack thereof — between a little girl and the first man in her life. Moving from the Distant Father to Good Enough, Demanding, Seductive, or Absent Fathers, she writes about Doting Fathers.

Secunda points out that girls whose fathers are enchanted by their every move, by each idea, each bit of humor, each attempt to make their mark, develop an assumption that the rest of the world will react with equivalent adulation, and are astonished when things turn out differently.

Samantha's father hung on her every word and rushed to gratify her whims as they arose. No dress was too expensive, no lessons or activities out of reach, no personal inconvenience worth mentioning where Samantha was concerned. She would call him at his office without worrying about interrupting, she would by-pass her mother, going directly to her father for party permissions. She flirted with him and charmed him, and he served up worship in return.

His marriage to Samantha's mother had lost its glow, and unconsciously he may have been trying to rekindle the excitement of his own early courtship and marriage, through showering affection and material blessings on his daughter.

His sister, Samantha's God-mother, was concerned and gave Samantha a National Outdoor Leadership School (NOLS) trip for her 16th birthday, hoping to shock the girl out of her self-absorption. The NOLS philosophy is to put people in touch with nature, the wilderness, themselves, and one another in situations where survival depends on team work. Three boys Antonia admired very much had gone on NOLS trips the previous year, and so, although she never would have chosen it herself, she accepted the present — mostly because she hoped to gain status in the boys' eyes.

She is still unwilling to disclose the details of her crystallizing and very dangerous mountaintop experience except to say, "I learned a lot from some great people, when I was in a very tight spot."

Samantha continues to be the apple of her father's eye. That will never change. But, the hypnotic power of his worship has been broken by her discovery and willing acceptance of the power of human inter-dependence. She has a new view of her classmates, and a new appetite for — and acceptance of — rigorous learning.

Perhaps this is the place to mention a small study undertaken in the late 1970's on the sex and birth-order statistics of easy and difficult classes in school. Educators and parents know that some classes are harmonious. Others clash. This study showed that classes acknowledged as difficult contained a higher than usual percentage of only-child girls or oldest-in-the-family girls. One must wonder about the role of My Daughter, the Deity and her relative, Deputy Princess, in discipline-difficult classes.

Deputy Princess is worshipped by a mother seeking a second chance. She may simply be a Disappointed Dowager, whose life never measured up to her expectations. Or, she may be a Detritus Dowager, the casualty of divorce and frequently replaced by the Trophy Wife. Vicarious satisfaction comes from watching her progeny, slender-waisted as she perhaps no longer is, sail off to conquer first the local party, next the ball, finally the world. The Deputy Princess may be expected to capture the social glories of a "correct" marriage and an "important" house. Sometimes, Deputy Princess — more intelligent or more accomplished than her mother — is clad, educated, and dispatched to bring home the professional laurel wreaths of advanced degrees or fame as a public figure. She must achieve, be the best, have high marks.

We have seen in earlier chapters the negative effect such pressures have on real learning.

When Deputy Princess is the daughter of a Disappointed Dowager, the older woman elevates the younger to heights she herself never attained. Then, in return for worship and material offerings, she often demands confidences about "how things are going in the romance," or assaults the daughter's purchased ear with "the injustices I've suffered."

Louisa, Deputy Princess, yearns to talk to boys. Like many beginners, she finds safety in the telephone. Every time she hangs up, her mother asks "Who was that? Did he ask you out? Does he get good grades?"

Louisa is inheriting the role her older sister Katerina has played for several years. When Katerina leaves for a date, her mother says, "Beautiful! At your age, I never had such clothes. Have fun. At your time of life, enjoy." She returns home to "Did you have fun? Did you kiss? How was it? At your age, I was never allowed to..."

In both instances, the young woman is both worshipped and adulated, while simultaneously being denied privacy and the humanity of her own perplexities. Her job is to be perfect.

Pawns in the Divorce Game Just as pagan tribes compete for godly favors by making increasingly lavish sacrifices, and by laying competitively magnificent offerings upon an altar, divorced and rivalrous parents often engage in a game of "Anything You Can Do, I Can Do Better."

The goal is to capture the child's allegiance and cut off the other parent. Escalating rounds of favor-buying spring from these spiteful origins. Sadly, these children are not courted because they are loved for their endearing and maddening human qualities. They are victory tokens to be claimed in a deadly game.

In school, these kids often expect similar wooing from their teachers and are surprised to run into behavioral codes and intellectual standards.

"I Want It Now" Kids with Push-over Parents

Some parents will say yes to almost any request in order to remain in the child's good favor. In this stance of inappropriate subservience, they are afraid to say no, to establish the boundaries of acceptable behavior, and to stick to their guns.

"He was just determined to take the car, so what could I do?"

"She insisted on going with the others. I couldn't make her an odd-ball."

"She said she only needed to use my credit card this once. I can't believe all the things she bought."

It's as easy to write the homework script for this cast of characters as it is to anticipate the quality of the schoolwork.

Quasi-Worshipped Children

These children seem to have been conceived and born to ornament the family holiday card, or give the parents an affirmative answer to "Do you have children?" — "We have an 8-year-old son and a 5-year-old daughter" sounds good, and a few photographs look splendid in leather frames in the library or silver in the living room. These daughters have new velvet dresses and these sons English blazers to wear for family pictures. Ready tuitions send them through the most expensive schools. Ski trips, sailing trips, or ranch excursions fill their vacations. But, the face of family intimacy the parents present to the world is surface-warm and substance-cold.

Benjamin and Ellen were born to just such parents: Edward and his third, much younger wife, Marjorie. The picture seemed flawless. But, why was Benjamin insecure and withdrawn? Why was Ellen mistrustful and manipulative? Raised mostly by an ever-changing parade of domestic servants, the children were trotted out for decoration, seated momentarily on their metaphoric thrones, and sent away when they were no longer useful. Their report cards were decorations — medals to enhance family honor instead of evidence of personal worth and growth. These children were treated instead of treasured.

A few years ago, a new kind of sneaker hit the market. Called Pumps because each one could custom-support the foot by having internal compartments pumped up with air, they literally vaulted to the highest possible status, despite their prohibitive cost. Needless to say, speedier than a Cabbage Patch Doll, more powerful than a new Nintendo game, Pumps arrived for Benjamin and Ellen.

When Edward fell in love with an even younger woman, his marriage to Marjorie disintegrated, and a peculiar custody battle ensued: because each wanted to pursue the next phase of life unencumbered, neither one wanted the children! Conceived and born to enhance their parents' status, and surrounded by trappings, these two were no better off than a pair of Pumps — fashion of the moment whose apparent strength and support was built only of air.

The First Grandchild

The first grandchild has a special position, no matter whether geography creates closeness or distance. Frequently, new grandparents hold on to the promise of immortality, sometimes even overlooking the infant's parents in the process. Eager for the sheer enjoyment of giving pleasure, which may have been economically or psychologically impossible when their own children came along, the grandparents' inclination is to idolize the child and memorize each word and funny saying, while sending or bringing torrents of clothing, equipment, toys, and treats.

Of course, a certain amount of blind, unconditional love is normal and a powerfully positive two-way force, but sometimes things go to extremes. Trouble doesn't show in the first few years, but comes later with "What did you bring me?", "I don't like that toy," or "You can't make me stop." Grandparents who have succumbed early on to grandchild worship lay themselves wide open to rejection and rudeness, as children try to establish themselves as individuals.

When a child is the first grandchild on both sides, the perils and temptations double. Wise grandparents will try to have a relationship WITH the child, enjoying, sharing, thinking, and DOING things together. This is possible even when they live far apart. Here is an example:

One grandmother who lived in California sent her New York grandchildren a simple cassette player and a "book-of-the-month." She would choose it, read it aloud onto the tape (making a few editorial comments along the way), and mail it off, including a blank cassette. The children became well-accustomed to her voice, and would record their reactions to the book on the blank tape and send it back. They developed a rich store of shared literature.

2. Where is the boundary between the appropriate and the destructive?

Our friends Daisy, Steven, and their three children, have moved to California from New York, where they used to be our neighbors.

Although the family is far afield from the performing arts, through a school contact their oldest child, 11-year-old Flora, was invited to audition for a part in a new weekly TV show. In this case, a look at the material showed that the term "well-written television script" was not an oxymoron. Even though she had no professional training, she was given a sizeable part. And, the scripts called for her to be the major focus of several episodes.

Daisy described going to the screening of the first episode. She and Steven arrived early, settled in their seats, and tried to size up the other viewers. "Will they appreciate her?", "Will they laugh when they're meant to?", "Will she actually be any good?"

The lights dimmed, the show began, and all of a sudden, there she was. She gave her lines with gusto and a natural presence. Then, as called for in the script, she laughed. It was her own wonderful, distinctive laugh.

"At that," Daisy said, "My eyes filled with tears, my heart came into my throat and I thought 'She's mine! That person on the screen doing these beautiful things is an extension of ME.' Then, I realized, 'No. She is her own person. Who knows where these talents came from, but they're hers, not mine. We live in the same house, and it's my job and pleasure to take care of her, but she's herself.'"

The show earned excellent ratings, sales of such spin-offs as t-shirts soared, and the run lasted nearly two years. Flora played her part with great pleasure. Out in public, she was frequently recognized and asked for her autograph. Once, she was mobbed in a mall.

Where is the boundary line between the appropriate appreciation and destructive idolization? Had Daisy or Steven succumbed as they watched her perform, they would have crossed the line. By seeing her as her own person — one to tend, cherish, enjoy, and set free — they gave their child and themselves the priceless gift of mutual respect.

Although she spent a great deal of time filming, she was held to strict accountability for her homework and other school obligations. The "minimum standard of acceptable behavior" at home remained the same for her as for her siblings. Being held responsible told her she was loved, not worshipped.

The world bowed to her professional achievements; her parents were proud but watchful. Her schoolmates were jealous and rough.

At one cast party, the performers and crew had each been given a baseball hat decorated with the show's logo. She wore hers to school the next day, and stowed it in her locker. Some other kids took it, stamped on it, dunked it in the toilet, and left it — a sodden heap — in the middle of the locker-room floor.

"Why did they do that?" she wailed, her cry of hurt as penetrating as her laugh.

Her brother said, "You shouldn't have worn it to school, Dummy. It's as much your fault as theirs."

"But, it's mine, and it's me. It's who I am. Why shouldn't I be allowed to wear it?"

"Maybe you should have saved it to wear at home or on the weekends," came a parental voice of conciliation. "Unpleasant surprises are the down side of having a high profile.

"If you want to be in the limelight, you've got to expect a few tomatoes along with the roses. It's better to face this early on in your life, because you're probably going to have an artistic career. You'll always have to choose whether and where to 'wear the hat,' and when to keep it in the closet. You'll have to make that choice over and over again, too. Each time will be different, few times will be simple, and having to make such a choice isn't fair. But, life isn't fair either. Everybody knows that. So practice up your choosing. With luck, you'll be right 50% of the time."

Sympathy, empathy, support, trust, and respect shone through her parents' remarks, just as schoolkid, street-smarts shone through her brother's off-hand, on-target retort. While none were worship, all accommodated admiration.

3. What are the emotional and educational results of being worshipped?

Children on pedestals, far from feeling safely loved and free to fulfill themselves, are prey to:

loneliness

perplexity

fear

anger and sadness

Loneliness

How can an idolized child feel lonely? We see throughout this chapter that to worship is to dehumanize. We know from the examples we have seen so far that dehumanizing means separation from others.

As a worshipped child loses touch with — or never develops — a clear sense of cause and effect, connections to reality grow more tenuous instead of more sturdy. Drifting through some private kingdom of privilege, other people's realities seem off in the mist, beyond the boundaries. In *Camelot*, the musical dramatization of the King Arthur story, Arthur and Guinevere capture the isolation and boredom of the worshipped in their duet, "What do the simple folk do?"

Sometimes, these worshipped children try to call through the fog — try to reach those ephemeral other people, who sometimes do not hear and often do not understand the cry for connectedness. They lose touch with family, friends, the satisfaction of a hard job well done, and, ultimately, with their true selves.

Perplexity	Wondering "What is it that other people know about me that I don't see in myself?", some worshipped children are confused by adulation. Others swell with entitlement and are annoyed when the rest of the world expects hard work and fair play from them. Deities don't pay income taxes. Lilies of the field toil not, neither do they spin. These children chant the litanies:

"If it's hard, I shouldn't have to."

"Rules are for others."

"But I want it now."

Perplexity results when the rest of the world doesn't provide assistance, recognition, and immediate gratification.

Fear	Fear is a frequent flyer in the underbelly of worship. Children who are worshipped for their functions — for what they can achieve or deliver — constantly worry:

"Who will love me if I blow it?"

"Maybe I'm not as smart (athletic, knowledgeable, popular, musical, fill in the blank) as everyone thinks. When will they find out?"

All children test the limits. Worshipped children, expecting more, test harder. When they can push the boundaries back, their sadness is born of realizing "My parent (teacher, caregiver) has turned the power back to me." This is profoundly terrifying: "I — young, chaotic, and turbulent — am the one in control." As we will see almost immediately, sadness, anger, and reluctance, with their diminishing of learning, arise in children who can usurp adult authority.

Anger and Sadness	These are flip sides of the emotional coin in many worshipped children. In seeming contradiction, depression may grow from too much power and too

little accountability for one's actions. A guidance counselor at Johns Hopkins University, describing the high incidence of depression (and such depression-related behaviors as substance abuse) among favored young people, talked about their established expectations that somebody would always be there to fix things up.

He started with the example of the child who was habitually late getting out of bed, despite an alarm clock and shoulder-shakes from a diligent mother. When the child appeared, late, did he have to choose between going without breakfast, or eating, missing the bus, and then having to walk to school? No. "I'd hate to have him go hungry," confesses the mother. "I say 'Never Again,' but I give in and drive him." Or, "This is the day of the big test. His teacher gets so annoyed when he's late. I don't want his grade to be lowered."

Perhaps this child, once in school, realizes his homework is back on the bureau. What happens? A phone call to the mother produces a drop-off. Perhaps this child is suspected of being part of a forbidden activity at school. When the parents are called in to talk about it, they say, "Not my kid!" Suppose a teenager gives a party when his parents are out, and beer is consumed. Other parents and school authorities are upset. These parents say, "We'll cover for you, if you promise never to do such a thing again."

Seeming support and ready provision of excuses rob the child of the power of rebellion and misbehavior. The child interprets this to mean that his or her transgressions aren't worth a reaction. Infractions of the rules are no more than flying marshmallows.

Depression is often rooted in helplessness. Not being able to get a reaction is powerlessness personified. When parents separate their children from the machinery of cause and effect, they sever the connection between power and responsibility.

Worshipped children are often sad because their self-concept is stolen away, replaced by a perfection which exists in the mind and eye of the beholder. Thus, pleasing the beholder is the only way to confirm growth or worth. Trying to be totally pleasing is an unattainable goal. People who are kept from setting and reaching their own goals become sad and angry. Their learning mirrors their emotional stances.

"Cornucopia Kids" (a phrase coined by psychologist Bruce A. Baldwin), who have been totally provided for by their parents, feel shocked when the real world doesn't continue to shower them with goods. They feel sadness that such a cozy time must end. They are angry at their parents who didn't warn and prepare them, at institutions or employers who hold them to account, and at themselves for not being able to maintain and continue their previous comfort level and idealized status.

Inside children who experience the loneliness, perplexity, fear, anger and sadness of being worshipped, emotional chaos replaces the security which could have been established by firm boundaries, strong leadership, and real love.

4. Can we break maladaptive patterns without breaking spirit?

The answer is an unqualified yes. Above all, we need to help these children exchange fantasies of personal omnipotence for bonds to other people.

We need to help them deliver an honest day's work, know themselves as people, and see others as people — not possessions. The next two sections provide specifics.

Ten Tips for Moms, Dads, Nannies, Grannies, Grandfathers, Teachers, and Other Concerned Adults

Each of the following — appropriate for all children but deserving special emphasis for children on pedestals — are designed to bring these kids into the real world of cause and effect, shared goals and responsibility, and connectedness to one another.

1. Children need the responsibility of regular work at home and at school. Emptying the trash, sorting the recycling, feeding the dog or the class guinea pig are chores which make life run smoothly. Even very young children can be given such opportunities and expectations. Sparing a child makes an automatic separation from others: participation is powerful glue.

One family I visited recently has what they call a "Waffle Tax." On Saturday morning, their father makes delicious waffles for breakfast. One time, long ago, the children disappeared after breakfast to watch TV. Asked if they would like to come help with some chores, they said, "No, thanks." Their father levied the Waffle Tax.

2. Beware of littering kids' paths with unearned rewards. Treats are one thing; by definition, they are happy surprises. Everyone needs one once in a while. But, children who expect to have all their wishes instantly gratified are set up for nasty shocks in school and outside the family. Having to choose WHICH kind of candy to get at the movies, having to wait until the weekend to watch TV, and waiting for the nearby birthday to get the bike — instead of buying it that day at the sports store — are sensible ways for adults to love and to give without being destructively indulgent.

3. Financial responsibility begins early. Each family deals with the question of allowance differently, but having predictable amounts of income helps kids plan. In our family, for example, our children were responsible for saving up during the winter for half of their own ski-tow tickets for our week of spring skiing. We posted a list of household jobs and their respective wages, each child estimated how much had to be earned, and on the Sunday before departure, we matched their earnings dollar for dollar. The message was clear: If you want to ride, work. If you prefer to climb the practice slope, that's your privilege.

4. Model respect for others and assume your children will follow the example. Most times, they understand without explanation. They are also snake-tongue quick at spotting inconsistency between what adults say and do. Parents who preach caring while snickering at ethnic jokes are teaching the lesson that respect is temporary and superficial.

5. Kids need to experiment and try new things, sometimes dropping them and continuing on to another beginning. But, they also need to know the feeling of working through to the end and tasting the satisfaction of completion.

This happens when adults lay out a long-term project for young and old to do together. One mother asked her kids to help move the woodpile closer to the door, so it would be easier to bring in firewood during the winter. In three Saturdays, the job was done. All winter, they reaped the benefits.

One child made a calendar for her parents for a present. Every month, she would collect something which represented that time of the year. Then, she made some illustrations, charted in the correct days and numbers for the forthcoming year, and proudly gave it to them for Christmas.

6. By setting out to learn something new themselves, adults model for kids what to do when things go awry. The father who struggles over computer commands, makes mistakes, and then masters the code is showing his children that failure is often the beginning, not the end. What better lesson can a young person learn?

7. Consistent with all the above, children need to be accountable for their own actions and behaviors. "Everyone who has shared in sorting the Saturday laundry may watch an extra half-hour of TV tonight."

8. Cooperative projects bind children in to adult activities and to affections shared between generations. "We need to clean up the den, so Granny can spend the night on the sofa bed. Let's all do it together, and then we'll all go have an ice cream and meet the train."

9. Sometimes, we need to help parents pull the netting off the mirror, so they see their own behaviors clearly. Good intentions, powerful affection, and misguided attempts to be "the perfect parent" may have slipped over into the pernicious stance of worship.

10. Teachers who become overly invested in their students' successes may benefit from similar mirror cleaning.

Six Specific Activities for Teachers

These activities would be appropriate for all children but are chosen for inclusion here, because — in one way or another — they speak particularly to the needs of worshipped children.

1. *All Together Now.* Through cooperative learning and simulation games, a child becomes a member of a group or part of a situation. Those interested in finding out how cooperative learning works should read *No Contest: The Case Against Competition* by Alfie Cohen. Cohen deals with both school and home situations. The example that sticks in my mind is his revision of the old birthday party game of Musical Chairs, a theoretically playful demonstration of dwindling supply and increasing demand. As Cohen points out, the purpose is elimination, ending with one victorious and resented child sitting on the single remaining chair. Why not, he suggests, turn the game inside out, seeing how many people it is possible to fit on one chair, rewarding inclusion and original strategy.

Simulation games, at home or at school, and now frequently on the computer, give children opportunities to play many different kinds of roles and to see the consequences of their actions. One word of caution: Children may get so caught up in the simulation that they confuse it for reality. This may be particularly true of a worshipped child, accustomed to being placed on the pedestal by adults or on the fringes by peers. These children need to be reassured that they will have chances to shift roles and change positions.

I once taught a brilliant boy named Eddie. An only child of two research scientists, Eddie was groomed in mathematics and science from his earliest days. He became a remarkably high academic achiever with low to non-existent social skills. In fourth grade, his class began a simulation game to accompany their studies of the Middle Ages. Students drew slips of paper to find out their identities. Eddie became one of the serfs. He tolerated this demeaning position as long as he could, but one day he could bear it no longer and he bit the simulation Lord on the forearm, drawing blood. Had everyone been reminded that the roles would shift weekly or every two weeks, Eddie might have been saved from himself.

2. *With Love From Us.* This can work at school, at home, on weekends, in the neighborhood, or anywhere at all. Collect a "cool" group of kids and give them a project. The group can — and ideally will be — multi-aged. Let them know the overall duration of the project — whether it will be for a weekend, a week, or six weeks. Have the end goal and celebration clearly in mind: "When we have put together a doll house for the day care center, we will have a pizza party."

One neighborhood group I saw decided to make a tabletop model of a Native American settlement. In order to do this, they had to make many decisions: what they wanted to depict, the size of the final project, which materials were at hand and which must be found or bought, how they would transport the model to the church/Sunday school/day care center where it would be displayed, and the best location and method of permanent display.

This group, roughly ages 9-13, had never worked together before. Three parents volunteered to help on Saturday mornings from nine until noon for four weeks. The ground rules for participating were that each child had to bring one fact about a Native American custom which could be demonstrated in the model, and one idea for raising five dollars to pay for materials.

Accustomed to being at the center of the stage, Courtnay had never done anything like this in her life. She wasn't particularly good with her hands, but when she saw which other children were part of the project, she was eager to join the team. The custom she wanted to depict was barter, and her idea for raising money was a Knowledge Fair — a card table set up outside the post office with slips of paper or index cards, each containing an interesting and little-known fact. At a quarter a draw, twenty facts would raise five dollars. Her ploy was so successful that they had fifteen dollars by the end of the first day, and put the surplus in the treasury as a foundation for the next project.

Enjoyment of cooperation, connectedness, and other people's ideas are a benevolent contagion traveling airborne from extra-curricular activities to classroom situations.

3. *How Do You Do.* With a group of four, pick an area of interest the whole class shares. Brainstorm the known information, generate questions to gather new facts, then ask the group to design a board game. The game should include elements of chance, rewards for information, opportunities for strategy, and perhaps currency or Chance Cards. This allows the worshipped kid to plot and strategize with the others, and also to become a participant in chance. These are catapults for excitement and learning.

4. *Winds.* Throughout time, the wind has meant different things to different cultures. Sometimes malevolent, sometimes the messenger of bounty, the wind — invisible — leaves its mark on our planet.

The purpose of this exercise is to help children explore some different roles winds play, and to see how knowledge from various disciplines can weave together. Through poetry, mythology, navigation, and fairy and folk tales, the "personalities" of each wind come to life. For example, we know that the West wind is as favorable to sailors as the East wind is treacherous. The North wind is as powerful as the South wind is gentle. *Old Mother West Wind, East of the Sun and West of the Moon, Hiawatha,* and a poetry book titled *The Attic of the Wind* — plus the weather segments of the morning news — provide excellent launchpads for thinking about this. Each child in the family or at school then adopts one of the winds or invents a totally new one, and finds a way to introduce that wind to the rest of the group.

One student combined hibernation with the wind. Here is his poem:

The Return of the Bear
With hairy paws
The wakening Bear
Hangs garlands

Of woodland roses
On the walls of the forest
Sprinkling them with water
From the springtime sea.

Where went you, Bear
In your seeming sleep,
To the sunless kingdom
Under the earth
Where the souls of the dead
Whisper their journey's events
And wait for others to come?

Welcome, Bear,
From your winter's dreaming travels
To sunshine
And shadows of the earth
The morning tang
And the wind that blows
From the South.

5. *Listen Up.* Cast one child — in this instance, the worshipped child — in the role of the director, who is to choose four actors. Together the group of five students chooses a story to portray. Under the director, the actors decide what form to use: skit, satire, a group poem, or serial recitation. They practice and present to the larger group.

Casting the worshipped child in the role of director may initially seem to be a reinforcement of just the tendencies we are trying to correct, but a second look reveals the opportunities and obligations. The director doesn't appear or perform. In order to do the job, the director must have a clear idea of the overall shape and purpose of the production, and enlist the support and cooperation of the actors.

6. *Moccasin Mile.* The proverb tells us that to understand another person, we need to walk a mile in his (her) moccasins.

Children who have been idolized often have no idea that other kids struggle to do seemingly simple things. Here are some books to offer the worshipped child. Ask for a report to the whole group on the content and message.

Keeping A Head in School, written by Dr. Mel Levine, is a clear description of learning differences, written for students. Although intended for a juvenile market, I have found it right on target for both parents and teachers. Worshipped children profit from reading short selections or the whole book, depending on their ages.

About Dyslexia: Unraveling the Myth is a short (47 pages) book delineating dyslexia at twelve successive age levels, each depiction being a tiny case history. Students from fourth grade on up have told me that it really helped them understand their friends, siblings, or themselves.

ONE CHILD'S STORY
Feet of Clay

Clayton is the youngest of three children in his family. His brother and sister are close in age, and family friends and contemporaries describe them as "joined at the hip." Their preferences and approaches to life are entirely compatible. This sounds great, but actually made life difficult for their mother: they closed ranks and ganged up on her.

Although she has a wide artistic streak, Pam was trained as a banker, having majored in economics at college. Before their children were born, she and her husband had decided she would stay at home and raise them herself. She resigned from the bank and exercised her considerable artistic talent by starting a custom-order, hand-painted tile business. As the children grew older, their interests focused on friends and athletics. They turned to one another for support more than to Pam. They joked about her business, teasing her with "Bubble, bubble, tile and trouble." But, the teasing had an edge and hurt her feelings. She often felt left out, but felt silly admitting such a thing to her husband.

When the older two were 10 and 12, along came Clayton. His personality was in tune with his mother's, and Pam's smile came from the inside for the first time in many years. She worshipped him. It was his picture she wore in her heirloom locket, and one year — not realizing the signal they were sending — their holiday card was a picture of Clayton in his red pajamas, wearing a long, tasseled night cap. It wasn't until a friend commented that they realized with horror how they had slighted the other children, absented themselves, and placed Clayton front and center.

The boy showed early artistic talent in some ways that came straight from Pam, and in some ways were like the talents Jack, his father, had stifled in himself. Although artistic, he was also a physically active and well-coordinated child. He was very close to his mother and was also interested in everything his father did, which flattered Jack. Pam, Jack, and Clayton became a trio, in counterpoint to the older children's duo. From the way they arranged the seating in the car and at the dinner table, it was plain that Clayton had favored status. Misbehavior didn't dislodge him from the catbird's seat.

Everyone expected school to be easy for Clayton. But, it wasn't. He was frequently rebuked for impulsiveness. He called out when he felt like talking; he demanded attention and immediate gratification. The word "wait" seemed to be missing from his school vocabulary.

By third grade, Clayton was on poor terms with his classmates, turning his quick tongue on them, wounding them with sarcasm and seeming contempt. He drew on his wide, deep store of general information in class discussions to make himself look smart, belittling the others by comparison.

That year, his class put on a production of *Peter Pan*. Clayton volunteered to make the swords for the pirate battle. Although his teacher worried at turning an impulsive boy loose to create weapons, he seemed so eager that she relented. Miraculously, Clayton made a dazzling variety of swords, daggers, and cutlasses out of cardboard covered with foil. He brought them in to school, carefully laid between layers of cardboard. After they were used in rehearsal, he carefully replaced them so they would be ready for the next performance. This gentle fairness was a new side of the impulsive and rather cruel child his teachers and classmates had seen before. When the teacher commented on this to Pam and Jack on the day of the play, they said, "You see. We were right. He's always been that way."

In sixth grade, he entered an electrical model of his own design in the school Science Fair. His parents had helped him with the display mount, but otherwise the work was his. Clayton and his parents were sure he would win first prize. But, when the awards were given, he didn't even earn honorable mention. The exhibits were left up overnight so the younger children could see them in the morning. No one knows for sure who tore the wires out of the winning entry, or who defaced the exhibit cards.

Pam and Jack expressed horror at the vandalism, but also anger at the judges and the judging. "It wasn't fair." Several weeks later, when the school authorities seemed intent on finding out the identity of the vandal, Clayton's parents made a $500 contribution to the school's discretionary fund, with a note saying they hoped it could be earmarked for science projects.

By the time Clayton reached high school, his siblings had finished college and graduate school, and were living on their own. Pam and Jack had separated. She went back to banking, and he found a girl friend. Clayton had plenty of free time and finally found a group of friends, though they were not the kind of kids a parent would choose.

In October of Clayton's senior year, there was a mysterious vandalism of their neighbor's house up at the lake. The cottages were closed for the winter, but someone had gone into this particular one, removed all the light bulbs from their sockets, and crushed them on the rug in the living room. The saucers from the pantry had been sailed against a tree in what must have been a wild frisbee game, every piece of furniture (beds, sofas, chairs) was turned upside down, and a framed print from over the fireplace was taken down and impaled on one of the legs of the upside-down sofa. The contents of the few boxes of cold cereal, probably left there by mistake, were sprinkled over the up-ended furniture, and someone had defecated in the fireplace.

Clayton swore he was innocent and that he had been with his girlfriend. He begged his mother to keep his whereabouts secret, saying his girlfriend had snuck out to be with him against her parents' wishes. Pam lied and provided an alibi. Jack seemed relieved that she was taking care of things. But, the older kids were angry. "You always let him get away with murder. He was up at the lake. He brought me back a Grateful Dead record I had left there last summer. I told him I hadn't meant to leave it behind and asked him to bring it back if he happened to be there. Come on, Mom, see him for who he is, for once. Take him down from the pedestal and face facts!"

Confronted with the new set of accusations from his brother, Clayton, clinging to his denial, exploded, saying to his mother, "You believe him over me? Fine. That's the end of my trusting YOU."

Jack says, "I give up. I don't have time for this. What happened? He used to be a good kid, didn't he? Or, were we just fooling ourselves?"

Pam can't bear to relinquish the idealized image of Clayton she has painstakingly constructed. Nor can she reconcile his words with the facts.

Clayton — guilty or not — is off the pedestal, drowning in the loneliness, perplexity, fear, sadness, and anger which engulf children who have been worshipped more than they have been loved.

Chapter SIX

CHILDREN AND FRIENDSHIPS

Connection, Rejection, and Alternative Avenues

Some children make friends easily. Magnetic, they attract others and give back warmth in return. They are sociable creatures whose empathy allows them to match their interests and intensity to those around them; they share their ideas, and know how to have fun. They have high levels of social intelligence. This capacity amplifies their readiness to learn, and broadcasts openness to ideas and people.

Experience and common sense help us resonate to recent research, giving academic grounding to what otherwise might be a touchy-feely topic. "Games of 'house,' mock battles of schoolyard Ninja Turtles and other diversions of young children have come under intense analysis as scientists studying the roots of social skills find that ability in interpersonal dealings can be crucial for academic achievement and success throughout life."[1]

I think in the imagery of a braid: the three strands children interweave in friendships are:

what they have observed

what they are inside

what the circumstances allow

Children's friendships are theoretically voluntary and supposedly stable. In actuality, although strong relationships cast a warm glow on life in general, unsettling fluctuations are commonplace, and rejection is painful. A disappointing friendship is like a broken filament. The bulb doesn't light.

Again, from the studies, come four archetypes who share common purpose, but who offer particular skills:

The Leader

First boy in a group: "I want to play mad scientist, but nobody else does."

Second boy: "OK, you get to choose who the leader is, but you can't choose yourself."

The second child excels at organizing, initiating, coordinating, and maintaining group activities.

The Mediator

First girl in a group: "Everybody wants to be Cinderella."

Second girl: "Let's just play we're all pretty ladies at the ball instead."

The second child negotiates solutions, prevents social conflicts, or resolves them.

The Friend

First boy, as others run off: "I fell and hurt my knee and the other kids ran off."

Second boy: "Ouch, I hurt my knee, too!"

The second child connects with others, starts and nurtures relationships and responds appropriately to others' feelings.

The Therapist

Girl observing two others playing: "She looks like a friendly person when she plays with that other girl. I'll ask her if she wants to be friends with me, too."

This child analyzes social situations, and understands and reflects on others' feelings, motives, and concerns.[2]

These are the lucky children whose social intelligence is active and robust. They attach themselves to others, their timing — in conversations or in asking to join a group — is empathetic, and they choose or construct situations with a high probability of success.

Others — equally eager for friends — stand too close, try to jump in too soon, come on too strong, or choose the wrong words, driving other kids away. These kids need to be taught the external structures of internal friendliness, and need to practice them just the way other kids need extra practice with their multiplication tables. Feelings of rejection or isolation absorb those emotional energies needed for learning, particularly in a group.

This chapter will consider:

the glow of friendship

the ache of rejection

alternative avenues

The Glow of Friendship From the outset, let's distinguish between friendship and popularity. The former builds strong bonds; the latter, like a soapy layer of lather, can rinse away in one shower. Temporary, exhilarating, and potentially devastating, popularity — or lack of it — has a powerful effect on children's sense of their own worth, willingness to risk, and enjoyment of group activities. It is a wobbly structure. Popularity is measured in numbers; friendship is valued in depth.

Since children learn as much from their friends as they do from their teachers or parents, it's worth our time to look at different structures and reasons for friendships — friendships to encourage or friendships to discourage — all the while reckoning the effect of friendships on daily living and academic learning. Children who feel connected plug into the academic opportunities around them.

Some friendships are based on "birds of a feather flock together;" others rest on "opposites attract." Either can be profoundly satisfying.

Jack and Oliver like to play with action figures. Early readers, story lovers, imaginative, energetic, and humorous, they can play together by the hour — dreaming up situations, imagining confrontations, shouting dialogue, devising heroism, and touting triumphant finales. Their action figures (we dare not call them dolls) fly out of trees, leap tall buildings at a single bound, conquer undersea monsters, and speed away in fast cars. They are sublimation unleashed.

Jack also plays contentedly with William, a strong, silent, artistic type. They draw, paint, make masks out of paper bags, design menus, create collages, or make dioramas in old shoe boxes. Jack does most of the talking, but William contributes plenty of ideas, albeit silently. Non-verbal children are often extremely skillful in the arts, in athletics, mathematics, science, engineering, and, later on, in such fields as medicine. They are frequently talented as well as quiet.

Jack learns well in many different settings. William needs help with self-expression. Oliver tastes success in play, therefore anticipates it in work.

Some friendships have their roots in convenience. Next-door neighbors usually find activities they enjoy in common. Flocks of neighborhood children play stickball, ride bikes, shoot hoops, plan pranks, or pair off to dress their Barbies. Other than shared space, these kids may have little in common.

As they grow, they will go their separate ways, yet they will meet up with one another in later life with the same amount of affection or mistrust they had for one another as children.

These are slightly different from "forced friendships," in which parents who get along with one another throw their children together, assuming the younger group will be equally compatible. Usually, these situations result in armed truces, quiet sabotage, endurance, or sedation by TV.

Common-ally, common-enemy friendships usually peter out when the job is done, or the foe is vanquished. The kids in Amelia's school joined a competition to see which school could raise the most money and gather the most food and clothing for a Thanksgiving drive to help people in the nearby city. Kids who had hardly ever spoken to one another were calling on the phone, planning, tabulating, packing, list making, and laughing. Their school won. In the aftermath, everyone remembers having had a good time; they remember one another's names and a few jokes about who contributed purple socks, but the camaraderie born of immediacy has cooled.

In the Middle East, the saying goes, "the enemy of my enemy is my friend." Friendships based on negative structures usually have a rancid flavor and dissipate as the grudge loses its power. Peter and Joey had been best friends. They had a falling out over whose fault it was that the money they had collected for their secret club had been stolen. Before this episode, both boys had picked on Sammy, a smaller kid who had wanted to be friends with them. After the fight, when Peter found paint on his bicycle, he blamed Joey. In retaliation, Joey invited a delighted Sammy to the movies and for a sleepover on his birthday. Two weeks later, Peter found the money bag and called Joey. "Guess what?

I found the money. You know who stole it? Us! Remember we decided to put it behind the refrigerator? We can have the club again. You want to come over?" "Not right now." "Tomorrow?" "Maybe. OK. I guess so." Poor Sammy is out in the cold again.

Some friends are co-experimenters: they give each other courage to try new things. This can be positive, as for instance when two kids give each other courage to take that first stroke in swimming. It can be negative, as when they say to each other, "Nobody's home. I wonder what vodka tastes like. Wanna try?"

Some friends are sounding boards: they listen and pull each other back into line, or simply provide a constant standard against which to measure new people or behaviors. Children will often bring home a new friend, particularly one who seems adventurous or sophisticated, to see their parents' reaction. Underneath their bravado, they are begging their parents to be the same old fuddy-duddies. The parents are the scenery against which the child tries out the new character in the play. Friends fill the same slot.

Often, it's not a new friend the child wants to test out, but a new self. In our family we called it "trying on coats." At various times in their development, our daughters tested such roles as junior Mata Hari, arctic explorer, bored sophisticate, cheerleader, egghead, hippie, and rock star. Punk and grunge didn't enter the culture till later, but we got a taste of those with our son.

Through such experimentation, the kid discovers which "coat" is comfortable, and which binds, chafes, sags, is becoming or unflattering, gorgeous or hideous.

Parents need to be on the "identity-alert," because trouble bubbles when you say goodnight to a mini-Madonna, and forget to notice that by morning she has become Ruth Bader Ginsburg.

Friends either go along with the masquerade, adopting similar body English, or they are the standard of reliability against which to test out new identities. At some ages, or in certain areas such as fashion, they have more power than any parent. "Why are you walking like that? Do you have diarrhea?" stops a poseur dead. Sounding-board friends keep us true to ourselves.

Children are often wiser than we give them credit for. They have a sense of who they are, but need to confirm that identity by playing with its opposite — by dancing with their shadow sides.

Single-purpose friendships may be short-lived, as we saw above in the case of the Thanksgiving drive, or they may extend over a long period of time, but be restricted to one focus or activity. In the adult world, we see people who work together at the office supportively and productively, yet have no desire to extend the relationship into social or family realms.

A man for all seasons: a friend for all reasons. The deepest friendships overflow boundaries of single-focus relationships. These are friends with whom to share work, recreation, joy, sorrow, perplexity, certainty, fears and foibles. Such friendship, based on compatibility and trust, is a priceless treasure which glows with the gold of value and the burnish of constancy.

Parents and teachers want to encourage those friendships which build in feelings of success, which offer challenge or trust or both, and which keep the child growing in understanding of similarities and respect for differences. Friendships in which the child can stretch, laugh, and love offer the kind of social/emotional nourishment which expands the child's heart, soul, and mind.

What about undesirable friendships? One February afternoon, I went to pick up our daughter, Polly, who had been spending the afternoon at a friend's house. To my horror, I found the girls skating on a deep pond, on very thin ice, with no grown-up anywhere in sight. She was never allowed to go to that child's house again, though the child was welcome to come to us. An incidence involving obvious physical, life-threatening danger is easy to talk over with a child, and making a deal about "you can't go there, but she may come here" is an easy sell.

Harder are the subtleties of friends who are covertly snide, who mess with other kids' heads, or who lie, steal or take drugs.

Janella was always polite to grown ups when they were in the room, but would snicker and make mean remarks when they left. This kind of behavior can seem bold and witty to a timid or insecure child, yet is hard to catch. Dorothea would take her little sister and friends into her room and tell them the facts of life, horridly and inaccurately embellished. The littler girls were awed, frightened, and bound to secrecy. Except for the brazen lawlessness of some inner city situations, most kids who lie, steal, or take drugs do so on the QT. A parent may suspect, but have a hard time making a fact-based case.

When a child is hypnotized by such behaviors and temptations, adults are notoriously unsuccessful in eliminating the friendship. Such efforts simply intensify the bond. Instead, we need a three-pronged effort to:

substitute other activities and plans

dilute the number of occasions the kids share

ration their amount of time together

Patience will win out. "Hate the sin but not the sinner" is a good goal, and faith in the intrinsic nature and strength of the one who is being led astray will show and have an effect.

All of the situations described above influence the amount of energy a child has available for learning. The productive relationships enhance positive social/emotional stances and help children travel wide intellectual highways. Negative ones corrode the spark plugs which fire learning.

The Ache of Rejection

Rejection hurts. It also moves beyond the social/emotional realm, diminishing academic potential and success. Again, research confirms what we know from experience:

"Those kindergartners who were socially rejected in October, Dr. Ladd found, did only half as well as other children on tests of academic readiness when tested the following May. At the start of the year, both groups were at the same level.

"Being rejected in third grade predicted a poor academic showing three years later...

"And a study of 200 third graders who were tested again 12th grade, found that the most unpopular children at age 7 or 8 were twice as likely as other children to have been arrested or to have dropped out of school by age 18."[3]

This is the logical place to make the distinction between rejection — an active, overt reaction — to being neglected or overlooked. While the "invisible child" may be saddened by his or her fate, being unnoticed is far less painful than being pushed away.

Kids who are friendless wonder why. The energy this takes, and the negative feelings it inspires, dim the learning current or shut it off. Looking for some causes of rejection, we might look at ten classic patterns, remembering that suggestions for helping and coping come in the next two sections of the chapter.

⊖ Some kids who mistrust themselves — whose negative view is probably closely connected to issues we have explored in previous chapters — will anticipate rejection from those in the outside world. This colors their anticipation of what they will meet in school, as well as their individual anticipatory style.

⊖ Kids who are out of sync with their peers don't intuit the accepted code of group behavior and conform themselves to it. Here are three examples out of a large number of possibilities:

⊖ ⊖ Children who are gifted see the world differently, sometimes understanding at a different rate, sometimes in alternative depth and breadth. They may be beyond the group in their thinking, behind the group in their social skills, and apart from the group mark in sense of humor.

⊖ ⊖ Overplaced children, who are younger than most of their classmates, may keep up or excel academically, but not be able to make friends because they are bouncing on different developmental trampolines.

⊖ ⊖ Kids who are chronologically well-placed but developmentally young, or just socially immature and clumsy, are irritants to classmates who are just stabilizing their own social skills. Fear of contagion leads to outright rejection.

Lorinda is the oldest child of two professional, busy parents. She and her younger brother spend many hours with their grandmother, who is physically frail and totally accepting of whatever the children do. Now in fourth grade, Lorinda has dropped back to her brother's level and behaves like a 6-year-old boy. She sits on the floor with her legs spread apart and skirt high on her thighs. She sneaks up behind other kids on the playground and pokes them in the back or shouts in their ears. She picks her nose without embarrassment. She finds hilarity in *The World's Worst Monster Jokes*, a collection most second graders are weary of.

She and her brother still take baths together and have the same bedtime. She has not been offered any perks for being older, nor any incentives to grow up. Her trouble with her classmates simply reinforces her preference for playing with her brother and perpetuating her inappropriate behavior. The longer this habit goes on, the harder it will be to break; and the wider the gap, the greater her inclination to regress.

⊖ Kids who come on too strong may simply be rough and not aware of their own strength. They may be mean. They may be bullies. Other kids will often placate them, but this is surface friendship offered out of fear.

Rough kids may be struggling with some of the issues covered in the chapter on anger — they may be compensating for fear or low self-concept by gaining physical dominion over a situation, or they may be modeling behavior they have seen in others they admire...or must be subservient to.

Mean kids engender fear and dislike. Hugh took Cathy's kitten and sealed it up in a shoe box. He laughed at her tears, and reacted to her threat of telling on him by threatening to throw the box in the trash masher if she told.

Bullies are cowards underneath, but this is hard for the bullies' victims to believe. The bigger the reaction the bully gets in terms of power pay-off, the longer the harassment will continue and the more intense it will become. Shutting off the bully's satisfaction stops the problem.

⊖ Kids who are sneaky may get power — but not friendship. They may be manipulative, dishonest, fickle, or selfish.

Ginny was a classic manipulator. As deft as a pair of human tweezers, she would pluck people up and drop them down in settings of friction of her own making. Last week, she corralled Jenipher on the playground, pinching her fast and hard. When Jenipher started to cry, Ginny said, "Martha told me to do it. She said you were a zit-face." Jenipher ran to where Martha was playing with two other girls and kicked her. Martha hit back and soon there was an unholy free-for-all. The teacher stopped them. "What's going on here?" "Jenipher kicked me," Martha wailed. "But, Martha said I was a zit-face," Jenipher replied. Both girls were punished. Ginny smiled and offered to help the teacher.

Manipulative kids are so intent on controlling others, they lose sight of their own purposes. Sometimes, kids who have no control over their surroundings try to control their peers instead.

"I guess I'll just have to call the roll and ask you, one by one, if you were responsible for spoiling the new white board by using permanent markers," the teacher said. One by one, she called their names. One by one, they said, "No." She called Dougie's name. "No," he said, turning red and looking at the floor. The other kids knew he had snuck in early from recess. "Everyone has said no, but the fact is the new white board is spoiled. The tooth fairy didn't do it. I guess I'll just have to punish the class as a group." In the hall, in the bathroom, in quiet asides, the other kids tried to get Dougie to own up to the deed. He kept on denying his guilt. Finally, the teacher said, "I'm going to leave a little box on my desk. It will cost seven dollars to get the whiteboard professionally cleaned. I hope whoever is responsible will put the money in the box, and then we can move on." The next day, the money was in the box. Dougie's mother said, "That's funny I was sure I had left money for the dry cleaner right here."

⊖ Fickle kids hurt others with their fluctuating friendships and weathervaning loyalties. Mimi would often covet whatever new pencil, hair ribbon, or toy Susie had, and would barter offers such as "I'll be your best friend..." for a turn. When Mimi got the hot object, she would go off with Cathy, their arms around each other's shoulders in exclusionary paradise. Susie fell for this over and over again, until one day she said, "No, you can't have it. It's for me and Emily." Independence declared, Susie was no longer victimized. In her days of bondage to Mimi's whims of affection, she felt off-balance throughout the school day. Now, she is both steady and ready.

⊖ Kids who are selfish don't attract others. It's as though their solitary greed over a toy, a bag of cookies, or a pack of gum absorbs their energies, so none is left for broadcasting those vibes of friendliness that are magnetic. They don't see the point in sharing ideas, nor do they enjoy hearing from others. Isolation-booth learning is much less effective than that which springs from conversation and debate.

⊖ Kids who curry favor with adults are quickly isolated by other children. Tattle-tales and goody-goodies earn deep disfavor. And, although a parent or teacher may force another child or a group to play with a toadie, the minute the adult is out of the way, kids take their revenge.

⊖ Kids are sometimes snubbed from snobbishness. At pre-adolescence, when kids (even the braggadocios) are unsure of their own selves, they punish any deviance from the group norm. To wear the wrong piece of clothing can lead to merciless ostracism.

Today's newspaper carries a story of hazing in a mid-western suburb. The object of the torture was found to wear underwear from Sears. It was probably better quality than the norm from Caldor, but it was different, it was a chink, and the kids moved in for the kill. Pretty? Fair? Of course not. A common tale? Unfortunately, yes.

⊖ Kids who show weakness are often ostracized. Again, it is the uncertainty group members feel about themselves which makes them hunt their prey, striking at another kid's vulnerability to enhance their own stature. They may sneer at a socially weak student's academic work, hoping to ride reverse coattails, elevating themselves at others' expenses.

⊖ Kids who hold a strong point of view different from the norm may have to pay for their ideology through ostracism. A child who wears such religious paraphernalia as a medal or a head covering, one who is a vegetarian in beef country, a Girl or Boy Scout in drug territory, even a lone Democrat among a group of Republicans or vice versa, is marked as different. Difference and danger are synonymous to insecure children. All kids need adult teaching and example to avoid the shoals of prejudice.

⊖ Kids who are intellectually powerful are often quietly rejected. No one takes a poke at their noses, but they simply don't get invited to hang out with the others. This passive rejection is just as painful as its active counterparts, just as insidious, and hard to reverse. Loneliness takes a severe emotional toll.

⊖ Kids who are just chemically incompatible reject one another in what I think of as "no fault" aversion. It's mutual, and as long as it doesn't contaminate the rest of the group, let it be. We all have the right to choose our friends.

⊖ Kids who are wimpy, quiet, different, fearful, learning disabled, or wounded in one way or another are often pushed to the fringes of the group. As mentioned earlier, "invisible" children are more neglected than rejected. While this is still painful, it does not leave the deep scars of active rejection, but may dampen their participation in group discussions and lessen their overall availability for academic challenge.

Alternative Avenues

Not all friends are classmates; not all classmates are friends.

In *Janet's Repentance*, the novelist George Eliot said, "The first condition of human goodness is something to love."

In *The Member of the Wedding*, the young girl, Frankie, searches for "the we of me."

Loneliness makes people feel hollow, as though when they call deep down into themselves, there will be an echo from an empty chamber. Children suffer deeply from these fear-inducing and fear-born pangs. Sometimes, these children immerse themselves in schoolwork as an escape; other times they can't seem to lose themselves in a task.

Simply providing entertainment — or surrounding the child with other people — doesn't touch the deep, shadowy pockets of the problem. It is possible to be intensely lonely in the midst of a group, particularly if one is on the fringe or on the outs. Lonely or rejected children need feelings of success and experiences of connectedness. Children who have trouble with their peers need to be shown some other avenues. Here are some examples:

⊕ Kids feel proud when they carry out responsibilities. All children long to receive love and also to be dispensers of accepted love.

Having a pet puts the child in the position of giver, as well as receiver. We might paraphrase George Eliot and say the first condition of human goodness is to be needed. To be the dispenser of care, the provider of the basket-bed, the maitre-d' of meals, the ear scratcher, the stick thrower, or the purr prompter is to be the dispenser of accepted love.

⊕ Sometimes, kids who have trouble with age-mate friendships do very nicely with children who are younger or older. Mike is a gentle boy who, in fifth grade, still likes to play with action figures. He finds delightful companionship in the afternoons with Howard, two years younger, who lives in his apartment building. Both boys benefit.

Marjorie spats with her classmates but admires two older girls who live in her building. They have taken Marjorie on as their mascot. They show her their make-up, they teach her their music, they even play with her dolls. They are each having a chance to revisit childhood, while appearing to be simply kind to a littler person. Marjorie has "places to go and people to see." The danger here is that Marjorie isn't being seen as a person in her own right, but as a human action figure. To be an idol, an icon, or an amulet is to be dehumanized. To be a mascot is to be a toy.

Lloyd has joined a neighborhood chess club. Although he is the youngest member by a good margin, he is a successful player and well-respected member of the group. He has earned his spot. He is giving, receiving, and connecting as himself.

Some powerful friendships spring up across generations. Loneliness is a major issue for many senior citizens — people with stories to tell, laughter to share, wisdom to drop, and needs to be filled. As part of a neighborhood program, Jeremy is a Friendly Visitor to Isaac, a retired diamond merchant now in his mid-eighties. Isaac's eyesight is failing, and his balance is no longer steady. Twice a week, for an hour each time, Jeremy goes to Isaac's apartment. He changes lightbulbs, takes out the trash, writes out the grocery list, sometimes does the shopping, and walks along with Isaac to cash his check and do small errands. They talk. Isaac tells Jeremy stories about vast treasure, chicanery, generosity, secrecy and how he learned when and whom to trust. Jeremy tells Isaac about his life in school and at home. They have hot chocolate and hang out together, the way friends do.

Opportunities to volunteer are around every corner and can be found for young children, as well as those old enough to be candystripers. Many Sunday schools teachers welcome junior helpers. People who work with animals often welcome young assistants, as do people who work with plants, bushes, and trees in greenhouses, farms, nurseries, or flower shops. Many museums have junior staffers or junior staffers-in-training. The idea is to find what the child enjoys; then look around the neighborhood and see which person, what industry, or what store is a good match; and inquire.

Mentorships are a two-way enrichment, bonding master and apprentice in a time-honored way. In *The Unschooled Mind: How Children Learn and How Schools Should Teach Them*, Howard Gardner points out that two highly successful models for learning use science museums and mentors. In the past, the older person would share knowledge and know-how with the younger one. Of late, I have heard of some set-ups in which the older person teaches the younger one something such as mathematics, and the younger person teaches the older one about computers or such electronic mysteries as VCRs.

Ten Tips for Moms, Dads, Nannies, Grannies, Grandfathers, Teachers, and Other Concerned Adults

1. All children need and can experience friendship. Children who don't catch on to the ground rules of how close to stand, how loud to speak, when to try to join a group, and when to wait to be invited need to be shown some ground rules, and need to discuss the areas mentioned above. They need to practice: "If I stand this close does it bug you? How about this close? Can you feel the difference?" Help them interpret cues of body English and social signals by watching TV shows with the volume off. Family sit-coms, such as re-runs of the Cosby Show, work very well. The first step is to help the child discover that there are rules and conventions governing interpersonal behavior. Many rejected kids never realized that. Once they know the conventions exist, then they can start learning to conform their own behavior. Children who are comfortable with social ground rules learn more easily than their uncertain counterparts.

2. Expand the limits of friendships beyond the goal of being best friends with a classmate. Put the child in a position to give care and attention. The act of giving — and having the gift received — vanquishes loneliness.

3. Solitude is not pathological. Fortunate people enjoy their own company. They may read, draw, walk, think, whistle, speculate, practice, or innovate. They are deeply content. Out of contented solitude come many dazzling creations. Children are born into the world knowing how to enjoy their own company. Constantly surrounding them with other people steals away an innate gift. While friendships are important, the meaningful ones aren't measured by how many people are involved, how many playdates there are, or how frequently the phone rings with invitations. Having one good friend is enough for many people, who consider themselves fortunate.

4. Children who are eager for playdates, but aren't sure how to make them work, profit from being with another child on neutral turf — for a specified amount of time and for a stated purpose — rather than free-form hanging out. When Sarah had classmates over to play at her house, she would boss them from one activity to the next, share some things but not others, laugh shrilly, and finally burst into tears. Her mother changed the ground rules. Sarah invites a classmate to come with her on a picnic in the park, they play on the playground for about half an hour, then go to the children's museum for about 45 minutes, and then deliver the other child home. New friendships solidify with this kind of help. Expanding friendship means increasing confidence. Confidence fuels learning.

5. Games with well-understood rules are easier for some children than open-ended, unstructured situations. Having a club for chess, checkers, or card games opens up opportunities to associate on common ground, without having to be a politician to be accepted. It goes without saying that learning games of strategy is intellectually stimulating, and leads to generalized improvement in ability to anticipate, plan, and act.

6. Children who enjoy using their bodies can associate and be friends with others on athletic teams, in gymnastics classes, and ballet studios. (Yes, boys, too.) Some kids who use their bodies well in 3-dimensional situations have trouble with 2-dimensional academic subjects. They make friends across athletic domains more than across abstract intellectual ones. These children need to show themselves in the positive light of accomplishment to counteract the poor press they get in spelling, memorizing, or oral reading.

7. Children with musical or dramatic flair can find companionship and shared purpose in joining an orchestra or local theater program.

8. Computers may be helpful or harmful. The rejected child who retreats to electronic privacy is hiding and hurting. On the other hand, children who play simulation games — or who connect with one another on puzzles, projects, or electronic bulletin boards — may be able to experience connectedness without the interference of poor judgement in face-to-face contact. Establishing the connection is the primary goal. Once that's in place, the child can expand to situations requiring more complex social awareness.

9. Teach kids how to be bully-proof. Bullying is an enduring and highly under-rated problem in today's schools. Our goal is to help kids "Scotch-guard" themselves against the pain of being bullied. This means finding ways to keep the meanness from penetrating. Grounding ourselves in research, as well as in common sense and personal experience, we can blend our own thoughts with those set forth by Elin McCoy and Lawrence Kutner, to name but two:

don't give the bully an emotional pay-off

Tears and flash-point anger make the bully feel more powerful. Deny the power by staying calm and having a few rehearsed comments at the ready.

be assertive

Having practiced what to say, a child can respond to a bully with "I don't like that. Don't do it. I'll report you." Said in a calm voice, accompanied by purposeful walking away, may be all that's needed.

do something unexpected

Rehearse with the child how to go on the offensive. The bully is used to defensive reactions, so turn the tables. "Quit it. You can't have it. Now move." Role play in preparation, having the child take turns being both sides.

strengthen the child's friendships

There is strength in numbers. Bullies are more apt to pick on a loner than a kid in a group.

get help from school or community authorities

When the above tactics don't work, there's nothing shameful in getting adult support.[4]

10. Children who are dependent on friendships for their own self-worth are outer-directed, and are at risk for doing what will make them popular, or accepted, or just plain noticed. Peer pressure is a powerful force.

Children who seek friendships because they feel good about themselves — and want to share who and what they are — behave with a generosity which draws others to them.

Thus, it is important to know what each child cares about, does well at, and is interested in, and then to budget time, money, and emotional energy for the development of individual talent and interests.

Six Specific Activities For Teachers

1. *Gardens.* Help the children chart as many different flower names as they know from their own experience or from stories they have heard: roses, tulips, dandelions, lupines, or beanstalks. Talk about the similarities and differences, describe their physical appearance and their smell. Perhaps there are some good illustrators in the group, or perhaps some children could trace and color pictures from an encyclopedia or flower book. With children in third grade and up, introduce the Latin names.

Then, give the children a few examples of a silly, mythical garden catalogue. Here are three examples from a book, and three from a set of dessert plates someone gave me for my birthday:

BURDIBUSH: Egginestia family. The picture shows a long-stalked, feathery plant, whose blossoms are formed of little bird heads emerging from tiny nests.

NASTICREECHIA KRAWLUPIA: Calamatus family. The picture shows a plant whose flowers bloom the length of the stem. On second glance, they turn out to be inch worms and centipedes.

SPULATRED: Gusset family. Each stalk has two or three sets of blossoms made of spools of blue thread. The legend reads "Modest and unassuming, this plant belongs in every garden. Sow at any season. Makes a fine border."[5]

SHOOBOOTIA UTILIS: The ornamental growth on the long, spiky stems is made of work boots.

TIGERLILLIA TERRIBILIS: The flower shaped like a tulip in full bloom is formed from tigers — tails at the bottom, stripes going around, and cub faces looking inward at one another.

MANYPEEPLIA UPSIDEDOWNIA: This graceful, willowy stem curves outward, with blossoms dangling from its arched portion. The blossoms have green bases (legs and bottom halves of torsos) and blue blossoms (top halves of bodies — upper torsos, arms outstretched, heads with smiling faces).

Now, let kids invent, name, and illustrate their own plants. Humor is a powerful cement. Kids who laugh together are bonded.

2. *Masks.* Masks let us either conceal or reveal our identities. We can cover ourselves with Harlequin masks, or become Superman, the Queen of England, or a creature from the slimy deep. Often, children who have trouble with face-to-face friendships enjoy the art and process of mask making, as well as the anonymity and security a mask provides.

Help the children make masks representing characters in a familiar story, and then act it out. Or, let the children make masks from their imaginations. Have a mask parade, so each one can show his or her individual creation, and then put two or three masks together, asking the children to invent a story encompassing those characters.

3. *Tally.* The kid who keeps the statistics has a powerful position. If a child is on the fringes because of weak athletic skills, appoint him or her to be the tally keeper, and provide a big piece of poster board and colored markers. Let the group decide what items and events to keep track of: birthdays, lost teeth, soccer games. Arrange a grid for the poster and a system for recording, and ask "Tally" to make the entries on a daily or weekly basis. In Chapter Two, we saw how and why a parallel plan worked successfully for Jeff.

4. *On the Road.* Ask each person to make an individual exhibit of something of interest or importance. Plan a time for classmates to show their exhibits to one another, perhaps even letting them remain on view in the classroom for a day or two. Then, designate a few students to take their personal exhibits to a class of younger children. One fourth grade girl, who had been excluded by the group because of her immaturity, was embarrassed to admit she was still interested in dolls. She titled her exhibit "The Evolution of Barbie," bringing in different Barbies, different fashions, different accessories. It was a huge hit. A lot of the other girls, who still liked dolls secretly, were delighted to find a permissible path into what would otherwise have been babyish behavior. Charting Barbie's progress as an evolution was an easy out.

5. *Animal Study.* Let each student pick an animal on which to write a report. They should write about and/or illustrate the creature's appearance, size, habitat, preferred foods, daytime and nighttime habits, predators and enemies, methods of self-protection, and probable life span. Then, let all the children present their findings to one another. Then, pair them up and ask them to write a story telling what happened when their two animals met. How do two creatures who don't know each other get together? Children...and adults, too...may learn as much from metaphor as from direct teaching.

6. *Storytelling* is an ideal vehicle for joining different people together psychologically and intellectually. Those who sit together and laugh, cry, shudder, dread, and discover have a powerful mutual bond. Children themselves should have opportunities to be tellers as well as listeners. The oral tradition is a noble one, recently neglected in most schools. Tellers can choose stories from traditional sources such as mythology. They may prefer folk tales from cultures all over the world, or they may want to tell stories from their own personal histories. Like other artists, they should practice before performing, there should be a special setting or mood, and the audience must recognize its responsibilities to contribute to the magic by being attentive and quiet. Many story tellers sit on a special stool or chair, or have a special shawl.

One eminently successful physician tells about his boyhood. He was poor at athletics, but earned his spot in the pecking order by being the camp's championship ghost story teller.

ONE CHILD'S STORY

Margaret and the Hamster: Source and Resource

The office is imposing by itself, but with the committee of eight judges assembled there, it was awesome. These authors and editors had spent several months judging entries in a national poetry contest. Each of the fifty final entries had been numbered and then sent anonymously to each judge. By ballot, they selected the top twenty-five, then the top ten, the top three and, finally, the first prize winner. The vote had been unanimous. Now, they were assembled, ready to meet the winner whom they had invited to fly in for the presentation.

A young girl, barely 17, entered with her mother. The judges held out their hands to the older woman, who shook them politely and said, "My daughter is the author. I'm simply along for the ride." The young woman smiled, covering her shyness with what appeared to be poise.

After some small talk about the journey and the weather, they all sat down. The chair of the committee turned to the young poet and said, "I must confess, I'm surprised. I find it hard to believe that someone so young could have such profound thoughts about the ephemeral quality of life, and the experience of mourning. How do you know these things?"

She looked up at him, and without missing a beat said, "I guess it was my hamster."

"Your what? Your hamster? This poem?"

"Yes", she continued, and the story came pouring out. "You see when I was a kid in grade school, I didn't have any friends. Actually, I didn't deserve any. I was a razor-tongued wise-mouth. I was bored most of the time in class. I always knew the question the teacher was going to ask before she even got through her tiresome explanations, so I'd be ready with a whole bunch of answers. I showed up all my classmates by being smarter and faster than they were, and they took it out on me on the playground.

"Recess was torture. I was pretty fast for my size, but small. They could chase me and get me. They would make a circle around me and close in, threatening to cut off my hair, tear up my clothes, or smear my locker with peanut butter. The meaner they were, the nastier I got, and I can say pretty cutting things. I didn't hold back. Things were in a vicious circle.

"I guess the reason I didn't go crazy was my hamster. Hamsters don't know if you're sarcastic and if you don't have any friends. Hamsters only care whether you take care of them. I loved Hammy. Every day when I got home from school, I'd open his cage and get him out. I'd play with him and sing little songs to him. I even invented a birthday for him and gave him a party with extra lettuce treats. I'd tell him all about how mean the other kids were, how I hated them, and how I could get revenge.

"One day, I came home from school and Hammy's cage door was open. He had figured out how to unlatch it. That time, I found him safe. He was in the closet, hiding in my bedroom slipper. I scolded him (gently), asked him not to get out again, and put him back. The next day, the cage door was open again, and this time Hammy had discovered the bathroom. He had skibbled up the bath mat, run along the rim of the tub, and made a flying jump to the toilet seat. He was running it like a race course, faster and faster. I caught him up, kissed him, and told him how scared it made me to see him there. I took him back in my room and played with him all afternoon.

"The next day, I ran up to his cage as soon as I got home. He wasn't there. Following my intuition with dread, I went into the bathroom, and there was Hammy floating on his back. Dead. Drowned.

"My mother heard me screaming. She came, and we lifted Hammy out of the toilet. She got a soft, down mitten, and we slipped his body into it. Then, we put the mitten in a box, and dug a hole for the box outside. She said I should be the one to put the dirt over the box. For a while I just couldn't, but then, first a sprinkle, then a handful, then some spoonfuls. Pretty soon the box was buried. I put a circle of white pebbles around the spot, and went up to my room.

"I just cried and cried. I guess I howled, too. My mother didn't try to make me stop. She didn't tell me everything would be all right. How could it be? Hammy was dead. She brought supper on a tray and just left it there. I stayed in that room and just grieved. I don't know how long I was there, but it was long enough to let things run their course. I sort of knew when I was touching the very bottom of sadness, and even through my despair, I sensed that now I would start my climb back up.

"I never bought another hamster, and my mother didn't even offer me one. That was right. Hammy was Hammy.

"After sixth grade, we started learning more interesting things in school. I found out that there were some other kids who were smart, too. We did a couple of projects together, and one night one of them called me up and asked me to come over on the weekend. Things got better. I only had a few friends, but that's all anyone needs. Gradually, I learned to like some of them, and I could tell they liked me. After a while, probably nearly a year, I felt like I could trust them, and one day I told them the story about Hammy. For my birthday, one of them drew a picture of a hamster. They wrote my name and Hammy's and the year he lived and died. They put it in a frame. I cried when I opened it. They really cared!

"I've always loved words; earlier they were my weapons, now they're my instruments. That's where this poem came from."

Chapter SEVEN

CHILDREN AND STRUCTURE

Shells and Bones

On the surface, this chapter may appear to differ from the preceding ones. Those have all been about emotions, and structure isn't a feeling. However, the support children receive from structure generates those feelings of optimism and willingness to risk with which the reader is intimately familiar by now. The absence of structure creates confusion where there should be the emotional certainty which supports and liberates intellectual growth.

Children need both external and internal social/emotional structure: they need shells and bones.

Tessie, now in her mid-80's, is a legendary teacher and mentor to other teachers and parents, as well as to students. Asked if she could choose one thing to guarantee all children, she said, "Structure. A kid without structure is like an egg without a shell."

A shell provides structure from the *outside*, confining what would otherwise be a spreading, gelatinous mass. How many kids today, lacking predictable order in their lives, drift and dribble away from opportunities to learn, because they don't know how to gather their own forces — or, in current lingo — "get it together."

Bones provide structure from the *inside*. The human skeleton keeps us upright, letting us stand, sit, walk, flex our joints, and maintain a consistent shape. Without bones, we would wobble and flop like water balloons. Intellectual bones, the kind we will meet in this chapter, give shape to learning. The ability to use language to organize thoughts — and knowing how to organize oneself in time and space — provides this skeletal structure.

The strongest structures are love, expectations, and standards. Ideally, home and school life each provide all three, reinforcing one another. That love is vital goes without saying. Realistic expectations communicate a message of belief in the child. And, standards equip children with codes of behavior for the classroom, home life, and the big, wide world.

When a child's home life is in disarray, paradoxically, it is important for the school to maintain expectations and standards. Of course, we must sympathize with difficulties. But, if educators also take the position, "Things are hard, and we are here to help you be strong and grow stronger," the child receives a message of faith and an offer of real help. For many kids today, school may be "their only island of safety in a world gone mad."[1] When misguided kindness dilutes expectations and standards, the message is, "Because your home life is a mess, you can't do anything. Your capacities are down the drain."

When the child's school is inadequate or unsafe, parents have to double their own efforts. Weekend or vacation enrichment programs, church groups, trips to the library or science museum, or a mentor won't compensate fully for unresponsive or low-quality schooling, but they can keep the child connected to expectations and standards.

We know that when love, expectations, and standards are missing at home and at school, kids find them in such alternate structures as gangs and cults.

As the structures of home culture, school culture, and popular culture mix with individual character, imagination, genetic endowment, and dreams, the shape of a unique human life begins to develop. Some kids seem to convert their everyday experiences to metaphoric calcium, building stronger and stronger bones. It doesn't matter whether they are kids from chaotic homes or military posts. They may attend huge or tiny, rural or urban, straight-laced or loosey-goosey schools. They may have soaring I.Q.s or modest endowment, be rich or poor, plain or striking, but in the words of the old song, we could say of them, "Your foot bone's connected to your ankle bone, your ankle bone's connected to your shin bone, your shin bone's connected to your knee bone, your knee bone's connected to your thigh bone," and so on — all the way up to "Your neck bone's connected to your head bone."

Connected, sturdy, flexible, these kids are well-supported by the interlocking bones which give an arm its length, fingers their strength, and a head its durability. Perhaps, it's not odd at all that when we describe someone of strong character, we say, "That person has spine!"

Some kids need LOTS of help with both internal and external structure; almost everyone needs SOME help. That's what this chapter is all about. For obvious reasons, the neediest are probably:

⊖ global thinkers, who see the big picture easily and may have trouble with incremental details

⊖ people with ADD, who need structure and have trouble establishing it themselves

⊖ people whose particular learning disabilities (differences) clutter their efforts to be organized

⊖ smart kids with school problems

⊖ split-custody kids who live half the time at one parent's house and half the time at the other's

⊖ neglected kids, including the affluent, who are left to their own devices prematurely

⊖ parents or kids who have never organized themselves around time and space

⊖ kids who are sad, reluctant, angry

⊖ kids who aren't held accountable for their own actions

⊖ kids whose families are laid back — who "let it all hang out"

⊖ kids whose essentially straight-laced families adopt the fake Bohemianism of "Ragamuffin Chic:" sloppy is cool, scruffy is noble

⊖ kids who are disorganized by nature and — like human confetti machines — scatter their ideas, as well as their belongings

⊖ kids who are confused by the world, their families, their school, or themselves, and may appear to fit one or more of the above categories, when in truth they are simply perplexed

Let's look at physical and social/emotional structures which match the needs of different ages, because we don't want bones to bear weight prematurely, nor should we put ace bandages or plaster casts on strong, healthy limbs. The following guidelines are representative, not comprehensive. Since they are cumulative, let's begin with infancy.

Structures and Infants
Physically, the human infant is totally dependent for food, shelter, clothing, cleanliness, comfort, and head support. Socially and emotionally, infants need to establish a sense of basic trust, which comes from having their needs met, from intimacy, and from the beginnings of loving communication.

Structures and Toddlers
Physically, whether shoeless or shod, this is the time young children discover the independence of loco-motion within the structure of their environments. Socially and emotionally, they benefit from the structure of predictable daily routines, exposure to language, the blessing of firm limits, the safety of understanding the word "No," and the power of making things happen. Being allowed to feed them-selves (fingerfood can be just as nutritious as food which needs to be shoveled in), pushing a toy lawnmower, taking the pots out of the kitchen cabi-net and putting them back in — all feed the toddler's sense of competence. But, being allowed to play with the best china cups and saucers dissolves the boundary between the lands of Yes and No, re-moving an important structure. As we have seen in previous chapters, limits make children feel safe. Se-cure children seek out learning.

Structures and Pre-schoolers
Physically, pre-schoolers need to exercise. Through running, jumping, splashing, kicking, chasing, pat-ting, dressing, and eating they learn their own bod-ies. They discover the structure of being bilateral, and their mirror-image left and right sides. They learn the structure of their five senses, and what each one's job is. Socially and emotionally, they learn to interact with others through language, sharing, and taking turns, as they absorb such con-

cepts as NOW, BEFORE, and NEXT. The child with sturdy language has a tool for communication and for being able to catalogue a personal universe. Children whose language development is shaky are tenuously connected to reality, planning, and learning.

Structures and Kindergartners Physically, kindergartners refine the different structures of both large and small-motor activity. They know which activities work best outdoors or inside. They have a pretty good sense of how much room they need for their projects. They can take from a pile the number of blocks they need to make their building, they can fit their bodies on their chairs, and they have a sense of how much juice fills a cup. Socially and emotionally, kindergartners solidify the structures which establish the boundary between reality and fantasy, they differentiate between themselves and others, and they develop an awareness of the group as an entity with its own collective needs. Understanding group needs and participating as a group member prepares children for classroom learning.

Structures and First Graders Physically, first graders accept the structure governing playground rules and games. Academically, they learn the structure of reading, writing, and spelling through the rules of written language. They learn a structure of order through numbers. Socially and emotionally, they move beyond random acceptance of magical happenings, as they search out the structure of cause and effect. They build academic competence and its companion — emotional satisfaction — on this structural foundation.

Structures and Second Graders Physically, second graders typically polish such large-motor skills as throwing, catching, kicking, balancing, and organizing their bodies in the structures of space. They begin to be responsible for keeping their work and possessions in their backpacks, cubbies, lockers, or desks. Academically, they polish their reading, writing, spelling, and arithmetic skills, bringing them to more automatic levels. Usually, their handwriting conforms by now to the structures of lines and spaces. This is the appropriate time to teach the structure of time. Socially and emotionally, they usually find or create appropriate outlets for excitement, joy, anger, or disappointment, although many second graders still burst into tears.

Helen was frequently in trouble as a young child. Her mother would tell her to clean up her room, but she would overlook a whole section. Her homework was usually sitting at home on her bureau, and her library book was apt to be in the back of the car. The contents of her desk and locker looked as though they had been stirred by a spoon.

Her teacher helped her organize her school materials. At a conference with Helen and her parents, she suggested some strategies for similar help at home. "Less is more" was helpful in this case. Helen had too much stuff. She was shown how to put things away by categories (socks, underwear, hair ribbons), how to keep things which would commute between home and school in a backpack, how to color code her school work by subject matter, and how to have the same number of hangers as she had garments. That way, if she had an empty hanger, she knew right away that something was missing.

Order came to chaos, actually and symbolically. Helen grew to manage her belongings and her thoughts, instead of being at their mercy.

Structures and Third Graders

Physically, third graders enjoy the structure of rules. Intensely interested in fair and unfair, they find safety and contentment in understanding and using "off sides," "foul ball," and "you're out."

With his small-motor function, Romero can make intricate Lego structures, cut, paste, pour, and write. Academically, he and his third grade classmates learn the structure of multi-syllable words, and use the structures of reading and writing comprehension: who, what, when, where, why, and how. They convert the simple structure of addition into the complex process of multiplication. They weave numbers and words together in word problems. They learn the structure of the four points of the compass and basic map reading. Romero and his cooperative learning group study explorers — using text books, biographies, or simulation games. Socially and emotionally, they carry out the structure of their daily schedules, classroom procedures, sequence of subjects, and interpersonal dealings.

Recently, he got in trouble for a classic third grade wickedness: establishing an exclusionary secret club with rules, dues, and a password. Talk about structure! Although the club had to be disbanded because the left-out children were very unhappy, the fact that Romero and his cronies had designed a whole social organization showed that the structures of who, what, when, where, why, and how had become part of their thinking. They will be able to transfer this process from concrete living to the abstractions of learning.

Structures and Fourth Graders

Physically, fourth graders can remember complicated rules of games even in the middle of passing or receiving a ball, or being caught up in the heat of the moment. They can move with power, speed, and certainty, diving across a classroom and landing in a chair one nano-second before the bell rings. They balance well and can use an implement while they are in motion. They can skate and shoot with a hockey stick. A year or so earlier, most of them could learn to skate OR to shoot, but if they tried to shoot while skating, they would fall down. Girls can learn to knit. Boys could, too, if the culture permitted. Their physical coordination allows them to perform complex tasks simultaneously, in a way which would not have been possible earlier.

Academically, the structures of decoding and encoding are second nature to well-taught fourth graders. They read with rhythm, for information, and for pleasure. In math, their structural sense of number patterns and combinations is strong enough to permit them to play with rudiments of geometry, and with two and three-step problems.

Socially and emotionally, they are like big puppies whose bursts of unstructured energy are a surprise to those around them, as well as to themselves. They are beginning to be interested in the structure of social conventions (dare I say manners?), and they like to know the "right way" to do such things as sort out a quarrel with a friend, explain a problem to a teacher, or have a conversation with an older kid. They don't always do it, but they like to know how.

Structure helps them move into new intellectual domains with precision, honing previously acquired skills while developing new ones.

Structures and Fifth Graders	Physically, fifth graders are like Eric Karle's Hermit Crab. They are rapidly outgrowing the structure of their childhood bodies. Because of this, they may be clumsy. They're not always sure where their legs end, or how far their arms can reach. Their previous sense of body structure doesn't work any more, because their proportions are changing along with their sizes.

Academically, their ideas are beginning to flood in new dimensions of abstraction, complexity, and rate. The structures they had learned earlier for story or essay writing feel cramped. They are ready for wider territories. They are ready to learn keyboarding and the use of a word processor. Intellectually, they are able to hold conflicting ideas in their heads simultaneously, wrestling with ambiguous questions. They need to learn new structures for organizing their thoughts as well as their written work; their possessions as well as their positions; and the sizes and shapes of their bodies in their classrooms, on the athletic field, and in the gym.

Socially and emotionally, they hunger for new freedoms and the safety of old structures. But, they still need affection and gentle touches. They desperately need to learn the structures for dealing with a new intensity of familiar feelings, and for dealing with brand new sensations. Adults who understand this deep-seated need can offer the emotional structure needed for intellectual adventure.

Returning to an earlier metaphor, a skeletal frame, made of bones of different sizes and functions, gives shape to a whole physical body. Social/emotional structure is an armature unifying the whole of many smaller parts.

As the human frame includes such different supports as leg bones, hip joints, spine, shoulder blades, ribs, neck, and clavicle, the structures we are talking about here include:

time

space

language

concept development

motor competence

awareness of self

awareness of what is outside the self

organizing of actions

organizing of possessions

organizing of ideas

anticipation of consequences

access to "executive function"

These — some growing from within, some imposed from without — are either nurtured or shattered by a child's environment at home and at school. Let's consider them one by one, remembering that most of the specific suggestions for help come in the following sections.

Time

Time is an invisible concept, accessible only through language. Some children don't pick it up on their own, and today many adults forget to check up on the child's understanding — or neglect to teach it. Children who aren't plugged into time have trouble planning their work, scheduling their free time and homework, planning in advance, or knowing how much or how little to try to do in a given piece of time. For example, such statements as "read for the next ten minutes," "this assignment is due a week from Tuesday," and "We're leaving to pick up Granny in half an hour" are meaningless to the child who doesn't have an internal sense of what ten minutes feels like, to the child who is shaky on the days of the week, or to one who is unaccustomed to being on time at home. Failure to stay on time is both cause and effect of trouble and confusion.

The kid who is disorganized in time will feel rushed, or pushed, or reined in, and generally at the mercy of other people's wishes. These lead to anger, reluctance, and other negative emotions we have explored in earlier chapters.

Space

Knowing WHERE things are and where they belong helps humans organize themselves in what is otherwise vast space. Through structure, we help people who lose things, who are naturally untidy, who live in more than one household, or who find physical disarray intellectually contagious.

Some very bright people have trouble with left/right orientation. As children, they may reverse their *b*'s and *d*'s. As children or adults, they may have to rotate a map to match their current physical orientation, before being able to use it for planning what road to take, which way to turn at which intersection, or which side of the buoy is safe.

In school, they may need extra time to lay out their work, they may have trouble using the left-to-right and right-to-left procedures in multiplication and division, and they may lose their way in text pages which are densely packed.

Language

Because we are all bombarded by language, and because children talk a lot, it is easy to assume that each kid's language development is on target. Unfortunately, many bright kids have unrecognized language weaknesses, which undermine their behavior and their learning. *Receptive* language helps us take in new concepts, information, and vocabulary. *Expressive* language is the structure through which we share our perceptions. Although the role of language in social/emotional development is enormous, we will limit ourselves here to some representative vocabulary of organization.

Such words as *if, until, whenever, the fourth, four, immediately*, and *each* are tiny sentinels of meaning. Because they look insignificant, they're easy to skip in listening and in reading. Yet, without them, the thinker cannot follow what's intended.

Terms of inclusion and exclusion (*all of the above, every other one*), terms of time and sequence (*now, not until, first, next, finally*), terms of spatial organization (the tall ones go *here, in a row, over, under*), terms of personal identification (*these people, he, she, it, we, they*), terms of description (*yellow, fuzzy, prickly*), and terms of command (*stop, no exit, enter here, one way*) are but a few of the ways in which humans use language to impose order and structure on movements, territories, sequences, and to sort out who does what to whom.

Children who have absorbed these terms through their receptive language, and who know how to use them in their expressive language, are equipped to understand how their world is laid out and to know what is expected of them. With this established, they can deliver the goods in class and in their independent work. Without this structural foundation, their thoughts parade "to the winds' march."

Concept Development This depends in large measure upon strong language capacities, through which children learn to explain in words what they have observed and absorbed:

"This one is bigger than that one,"

"If you pour too much water in a container, it will spill over the top,"

"Birds fly in the air, and can also land and hop on the ground. Animals walk on the ground and do not fly,"

"Giants are not real."

A central job of early childhood is to figure out the rules of cause and effect which order our universe. Some are visible: rubber balls bounce. Others are hidden: the supermarket door opens when a person approaches. Without words to explain, the child must assume it happens by magic, or that a miniature doorman with a beeper lives under the rubber mat.

Children with weak concept development — perhaps from language weakness, perhaps because their parents and caretakers are neglectful, or perhaps because they have low reasoning abilities — lack the structure which makes the world dependable and safe. They are cut off from that sense of logical anticipation which stabilizes their universe. The resulting uncertainties and gaps of knowledge make learning a threatening prospect instead of an inviting one.

Motor Competence

Competence in the large and small motor system provides a sense of security:

"I can ride my bike without falling,"

"I can get my key in the lock and open the door,"

"I can carry this pot of water to the stove,"

"I can write my name."

Minor accomplishments, these, for those of us who take them for granted. But, think what life would be like were we not able to perform them.

Large-motor competence allows us to travel the circumferences, diameters, and radiuses of our lives, physically prowling the terrain and boundaries of our environment.

In the small motor arena, automatically correct handwriting is a sub-structure which liberates the student's creative energies for ideas. Correct keyboard fingering provides the structural, mechanical skill for using a word processor.

These competencies free the student's attentional energy to focus on content rather than mechanics.

Awareness of Self

Awareness of self — as distinct from objects or other people — underlies the structure of the concept "I." Understanding and operating within the implications of "I" is a cornerstone of psychological development, a structure through which a whole self emerges.

This, of course, is a major underpinning of the ability to form, state, and defend an opinion, without which learning is simply parroting.

Awareness of What Is Outside the Self
The concepts embodied in such words as *you, me, we, they, it, mine, yours,* and *ours* form the structure of humanity's social contract. They govern our behavior to and with one another. Most conflict has a transgression of one of these structures at its root:

"He took my car,"

"You hurt me."

Although family structures are changing, and the word *family* is actually being redefined, people still rely on one another through friendships and kinships. Having a group to rely on provides one sort of social/emotional structure. Being relied on by others is equally nourishing.

Feelings of connectedness are fundamental to emotional well-being, and make the process of expressing ideas and listening to other points of view an exciting opportunity. Children with this emotional and intellectual stance thrive on classroom discussion and contribute to general learning, while strengthening their own conceptual muscles.

Organizing Actions
People who use the structures of when, where, who, what, why, and how to organize their actions can function smoothly and effectively. Remember Romero and his friends, who formed the secret club. People lacking one or more of these tools flit randomly and sporadically, wasting time, opportunity, intention, and intelligence. School work suffers, self-concept plummets. While some kids independently discover how to use the six tools, many smart kids need to be taught. Parents and teachers must assume this responsibility.

Organizing Possessions	People who can find their tools and equipment quickly can operate efficiently. Knowing where things are disposes of unnecessary questions. I think in the imagery of a tool belt: a loop apiece for a hammer, screwdriver, tape measure, knife, and pliers, and a pocket for nails. Many bright kids need extra help in establishing similar structures for their possessions. To be confident, effective learners, they need ready access to their equipment.
Organizing Ideas	Children need structure to organize their ideas. Particularly at times of psycho-social, developmental growth, they need extra help managing new rates of thought, new levels of complexity, and new forces of abstraction.

Young children with wide-ranging curiosity may have trouble "finding the main idea." All ideas intrigue them, therefore all are important. Older children need help, too. The nature of children is to be collectors, yet sorting out to get "the main idea" requires winnowing. A child who is still in the collector's phase will doubtless be a poor winnower.

Many children who do well in discussion — at home or at school — fall apart when they try to put their ideas on paper. This is usually because they have not been taught — or have been taught but have not learned — the basic principles for organizing written output.

This difficulty is a classic source of academic trouble. We will see very specific teaching techniques for addressing such problems in the section, Six Specific Activities for Teachers.

Anticipation of Consequences	To anticipate the consequences of one's wishes or deeds requires a clearly developed internal timeline. This temporal structure is like a social/emotional railroad track, on which one travels backwards from the present to the past, returns to the present, zooms

to the distant future, or chugs along to a time close at hand. Once more, we see the importance of time. Anticipation requires analyzing past events, assessing the current situation, weighing alternatives, anticipating consequences, and following one's plan.

People who act without anticipation of the consequences are a trial to others and a danger to themselves — a disaster in the classroom and maddening at home. The negative responses they get from the world undermine their faith in themselves. Often, they try harder, meaning they do the same things but with greater intensity, which simply makes things worse. Thinking in bits and pieces, they act in fits and starts, making little if any forward motion.

Access to Executive Function

Executive function is the intellectual and social/emotional structure which allows people to consider, plan, sequence, monitor, evaluate, and change their actions.

Neurologist Martha Denckla uses the acronym "ISIS" to delineate this uniquely human capacity:

Initiate. Can the person initiate a thought or action?

Sustain. Can the person sustain that thought or action?

Inhibit. Can the person inhibit distraction from without or within?

Shift. Can the person shift from one thought or action to another?

Executive function requires all the sub-structures of time, space, motor competence, language, etc., which we have considered above. Executive function is the cumulative harvest of their combination, and the foundation of autonomy, confidence, and intellectual availability.

What are we supposed to do about all this?

Ten Tips for Moms, Dads, Nannies, Grannies, Grandfathers, Teachers and Other Concerned Adults

1. Consistency is the epoxy resin of structure. Children who find consistent codes of expectations, standards, behavior, and discipline among the adults who care for them know exactly where their boundaries are. Children are confused — and become manipulative — when school operates one way and home life another. In instances of separation or divorce, although they may be temporarily pleased with their own power, they are confused by finding different standards at Mom's house and Dad's house. When their caregiver, their parent(s), and their school have three different codes, they have a hard time knowing which to adhere to.

When divorced, separated, or under-the-same-roof parents understand the devastating effect of inconsistency on a child's learning and living, they may be able to set aside personal differences to draft a common set of basic expectations and standards for bedtime, food, homework, sharing household obligations, and plain old manners. When these issues are pawns in power plays of marital discord, children pay the price for adult selfishness.

Some enlightened schools now offer courses for caregivers (nannies, au pairs and sitters also fit this category). In four or six sessions, participants hear about the value of consistency, effective methods of discipline, the how's and why's of language development, guidelines for homework, productive uses of unstructured time, and ways for solving problems. Each presentation is accompanied by an outline, and each session includes time for discussion. At the end of the final session, there is a party, and participants receive certificates.

The caregivers feel empowered. Parents can expect that consistent threads will run through the child's day. People at the school get to know the caregivers as well as the parents. Caregivers' feelings of school phobia wash away, as the school becomes a source of their own increased professionalism. In setting up such a training course, it is vital to involve parents in both planning and content. This avoids turf fears.

2. Sheridan's Tyranny. Harriet Sheridan, past Dean at Brown University, urged adults to help kids develop organization in both time and space. She said, "These are helpful in elementary school, useful in middle school, productive in high school, and vital for success in college." That being the case, the sooner we start the better.

This benevolent tyranny requires establishing a treaty with the child, including a regular time and place for doing homework; a regular place to keep all school materials; organizing those materials by color coding; and having a family "work station" with pencils, pens, paper, a dictionary, a clock, calendar, good lighting, and perhaps a computer.

If the child is part of forging the treaty, which can be renegotiated from time to time, it feels like choice, not coercion. The child who establishes these organizational habits early has solid structure for subsequent growth.

3. Clocks. Sheridan's Tyranny shows us the importance of organization in time. Thus, adults should be sure the children in their care understand this invisible concept. Time is linear — moving forward and backward — and also circular — repeating the minutes, hours, days, months, seasons. For this reason, analog as well as digital clocks should be part of each child's environment. Many children, introduced to digital wrist watches as small children, don't grasp the meaning of the numbers on the faces of the clocks. Children also need to learn to feel the sense of elapsing time. "How long were we at the dinner table?" "Please be ready in twenty minutes." Many bright, well educated kids these days need teaching and coaching in this concept we used to take for granted.

4. Calendars. Increasing the child's temporal organization, calendars allow us to chart invisible time on visible spatial grids.

Both at home and at school, there should be a big calendar showing several months at a time. Regular events such as Tuesday night hockey practice should be marked in one color, forthcoming one-time events in another, long-term assignments in still another, and so forth. At the end of each day, one designated member of the class or the family should draw a little rebus showing something that happened that day: an umbrella if it rained, a birthday cake, a basketball if there was a game. The item doesn't matter. What is important is keeping a personal record. Then, every week or two — or at the end of every month — the family or class can look back: how many birthdays did we have in the last two months, were there more rainy days or sunny days, how did the team do over the season. Anchoring personal experience with art work on a chart of time (i.e., a calendar) clarifies an amorphous concept, and gives kids a major structural tool.

Families with split-custody arrangements should have duplicate calendars. Neglecting to provide such simple aids penalizes the children for the parents' problems.

5. Ideally, we would follow Sheridan's Tyranny for organization in space by arranging for each child to have a work station at home, comparable to a desk at school — a central spot for keeping academic materials, and one which is associated with concentrated work. Some kids study well in their bedrooms; others don't because the associations of day dreaming, night dreaming, listening to music, or just goofing off are too strong. Some kids work well in the kitchen; others need quiet. Some can gather peacefully around the dining room or kitchen table. Each family will work this out individually.

6. Color coding. This is another way to improve spatial organization. Many bright children have trouble organizing their school work when they put it away, and finding it later. Color-coded folders, notebooks, or notebook sections — combined with pens in parallel colors — can help. Red for math, green for language arts, blue for social studies, yellow for science. Then, the child needs a backpack large enough to hold the collection of notebooks, plus the few textbooks he or she may need to transport.

The family calendar can also be marked with the designated color for a long-term assignment, with a line starting on the day the project is assigned and running until the due date. That way, a glance at the calendar will show whether the allotted time is part-way up, half-way up, or virtually gone.

7. With the child or children, brainstorm a list of "Confusing Concept Words." My classics would be *unless, whenever, until, each,* and ordinal and cardinal numbers. Write them on a poster board or large index card, and talk them over. Then, incorporate them in games of Simon Says:

"Simon Says unless I clap my hands, don't take one step forward,"

"Simon Says whenever I whistle, put your thumb in your ear,"

"Simon Says wiggle each of your fingers three times,"

"Hold up your fourth finger...Oops, you're out. I didn't say 'Simon Says!'"

Many children learn quickly in the pleasurably exciting context of a game. The limbic system strikes again.

8. In approaching a new task, teach the child to use the Five Questions, also mentioned on page 9:

What do I already know?

What do I need to find out?

Where can I get this information?

How will I collect and categorize it?

How will I use it in what kind of final product?

Lots of curious, intelligent kids with good attitudes stall out academically, because they don't know where or how to begin, what intermediate steps to take, and what to do with everything once they have it.

9. Use lists. Keep them brief. Check off each item as it is accomplished. Limit the list to twelve items. Longer lists are overwhelming, non-completion lead to guilt, and guilt spawns procrastination. Start small, taste success, proceed with pride. Limbic liberation!

10. Improve listening skills. Much academic activity, particularly in elementary school, involves listening. Explanations, procedures, and plans elude the child who listens poorly. And, if teachers today were asked to pinpoint one single classroom problem, most would say, "Kids don't know how to listen." So, maybe we need to show them how.

Teach the child four strategies:

make a mental movie
get a picture in your mind of what you are supposed to do, or what the character in the story is doing

repeat
whisper the instructions back to yourself: "get three crayons, two pieces of paper, a handful of paperclips and sit on the rug."

draw a rebus or jot a note
use math, art, or a note

ask for a repetition
"Could you repeat the last part, please?"

We adults should teach ourselves to give clear explanations and directions. Four hints:

start with the punchline:
"This origami project will produce a windmill."

tell how many steps there will be and hold up that number of fingers:

"There are seven steps to this project. They need to be done in order."

provide a visual aid:

"This outline lists the steps and shows a picture of the final result."

help kids keep track of where they are in the overall plan:

"Good, you're half-way there. Soon, it will start to look like something."

Clear explanations increase the chances for good listening. Most of us use too many words, creating clutter instead of clarity. For additional strategies, see *Clear and Lively Writing*, noted in the Resource Section.

Six Specific Activities for Teachers

The following activities and strategies dovetail with the six priorities in Chapter One. While they are of major help to kids in need of structure, they are useful to all kids, even those who don't appear to need help.

1. Children need both aspects of language: texture and structure. Texture comes through word play, listening to stories read aloud, exposure to literature, memorizing poetry, and creative writing.

Understanding the structure of language comes through multisensory training in sound/symbol correspondence; learning to read, write and spell; knowing the rules for taking multi-syllable words apart and putting them back together; recognizing the kinship of words through roots and affixes; and toying with homonyms (*steel, steal*), homographs (*present, present*), synonyms, antonyms, figures of speech, simile, and metaphor.

Common Ground: Whole Language and Phonics Working Together lays out actual teaching methods and lesson plans for teachers of children in grades K-4. It, too, is noted in the Resource Section. To polarize children's early reading instruction into EITHER whole language OR phonics is like asking children to shop with only one side of a coin.

2. *Six Colored Pens.* (suitable for children in third grade through college). Color can give a student visual clues for organizing intake from reading and output through writing. Here's what to do.

First, be sure the students understand the 6 *wh* words and the concepts they represent (*who, what, when, where, why, how*). Clear up any obvious or latent confusion about these words, then give each student six felt-tip pens in six different colors. Ask them to tape one of the concept words on each pen thus:

who = green
what = red
when = purple

where = blue
why = black
how = orange

There is nothing sacred about these color combinations. Use whatever ones you like; just be consistent within the school.

Explain that every well-crafted story — and every satisfying piece of gossip — contains these six elements. Next, tell the class a short story. Ask them to write briefly who it was about in green, what happened in red, when it took place in purple, where it was in blue, why it took place in black, and how it came about in orange. When they have done that successfully, give them a selection to read and have them underline the elements in their assigned colors. Then, comes the fun.

Ask them to each think of a story, take out six index cards, put the six colored pens on the upper left-hand corner of their desks, write one element on an index card in the pen of the designated color, and then move that pen to the upper right-hand corner of the desk. As the students use each element in their stories, the pens will migrate across their desks. At a glance, it's obvious how many elements have been covered, and how many remain. When all the pens have been shifted from left to right, it's time to write the story. The student should spread the index cards across the desk, deciding which element will be the starter, which the finale, etc., all the while being able to move the cards around until the story line is pleasing.

Some writers want to start with who: "A little shepherd boy with chilblains on his knobby knees..." Others may prefer to start with why: "Jealousy frequently leads to murder, so it's no surprise Isobel was dead." Perhaps one writer will choose when and where: "It was a dark and stormy night..." There is no right or wrong; it's purely a matter of author's preference, and with this system, the preference is well supported by structure.

Students who are making independent choices have ownership of their learning, and consequently meet their work with enthusiasm and pride.

3. *Shape Up.* Following the colored pens, here is a device for using shape to organize reading comprehension and written work.

Explain that almost all written work can be categorized into the geometric forms explained below:

A newspaper article, which starts with a fact or opinion at its apex and adds more and more supporting material, fits this shape:

A riddle or mystery story does the opposite. It starts with a mass of facts and details, and whittles down to the point:

A recipe or manual is simply a consecutive series and fits this shape:

History and literature either fit a diamond or an hourglass. Well-constructed classic novels start on the point, expand, and return. We might say this shape fits George Eliot:

Others, more abstract, begin with many facts, narrow down to a very tight middle, and expand again. We might say this shape fits T.S. Eliot:

Many people never enjoy the literature which fits the hourglass shape, but need to know it exists.

Then, ask each student to draw these shapes on an index card and tape the card to the top of his or her desk. Next, read aloud a brief selection. Can the students tell which shape it fits? Probably. Next, give them a brief selection to read. Can they spot the shape? Yes. Then comes the culmination.

Ask each student to take out the Six Colored Pens, think of something to write, choose the shape, and...begin. (These color and shape exercises were outlined for the first time in *Clear & Lively Writing*, which is listed in the Resource Section.)

The excitement and relief flooding the faces of kids no longer terrified at the prospect of writing is a miracle to behold. Their limbic systems are saying "Yes," they are fully engaged, and the switch is in the On position.

4. *Mind Mapping.* Some people get so flooded with ideas, they panic at the thought of trying to capture them on paper. These are the writers (student or adult) who blurt and jump, surging, sparking but not developing thoughts or narratives. Here is a way to help, parallel to the currently popular technique known as Word Webbing. Let's say the topic is Opportunities in Automation and Electronics.

Give each student a piece of paper, in the middle of which will go the overall topic. The strategy is for the thinker to free-associate, jotting down ideas as they occur. After ten or fifteen minutes, the paper might look like this:

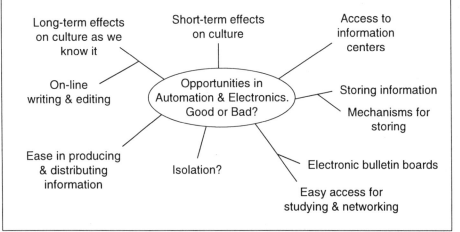

The ideas are now collected, panic recedes, and the writer can decide where to begin and in which order to present his or her thoughts. This system works well for global thinkers, sometimes called simultaneous processors.

5. *Outlining.* Teach the students the classic approach to outlining:

1.
   A.
   B.
      i.
      ii.
         a.
         b.
2.
   A.
   B.
      etc.

This system works well for students who think in logical sequence. Sequential and simultaneous processors — together — benefit from knowing all kinds of structure, not simply the one which fits their preferred mode.

6. *S.O.L.V.E.* This is a structural tool for organizing. It is an acronym for:

S = study the problem
O = organize the data
L = line up a plan
V = verify the plan
E = evaluate the match between answers and questions

This provides a structure and sequence which moves "studying" out of miasmal mists of confusion and into the realm of possibility.

ONE CHILD'S STORY

Joel and his younger brother live in an apartment in a medium-sized city close to a major metropolis. His father is a middle-management employee with a corporation which is down-sizing. Therefore, Joel's father is worried about his job. He works extra hours to prove his worth to his boss. Because Joel's mother is in the hospital for a protracted stay with a broken back — the result of an accident — the benefits package is doubly important. Fortunately, the well-equipped hospital is nearby, and the boys and their father can get there on public transportation. Everybody says how lucky that she need not be cut off from her family, and that they can get there easily for visits. But, under the surface serenity, things are bumpy.

Although he works many extra hours, Joel's father arranges to be home for at least one full day over the weekend. Together, he and the boys do the laundry, attend to accumulated errands, and shop for the upcoming week. Before and after school the rest of the week, Joel is expected to take care of himself and keep an eye on his little brother. Usually, his father leaves very early in the morning, so Joel and his brother eat cereal. At the end of the day, they put their frozen dinners in the microwave. Their father wishes he were home to eat with them, and sometimes is.

As a young child, Joel was a bright student and an early reader. Because he was so quick at learning sight words, his teacher didn't think he needed to be bothered by phonics. When other kids in the class were learning sound/symbol correspondence, Joel was allowed to do Tangram puzzles. His handwriting was labored and sprawling, but his teacher was sure he would improve and catch up when "it's important to him."

Before the accident, the family's routines were friendly and informal. The boys would have baths some nights, but not others. They would eat in front of the TV some nights, but at the table other times. Some nights, they would watch a video after supper, some nights they would take a walk, and some nights they would just go to bed. Their mother's style was reactive instead of proactive.

All of a sudden, she would discover the laundry hamper overflowing. There would be a flurry of activity and bed-changing. Or, they might have sandwiches for supper three nights in a row, and then stew made from scratch with fresh vegetables, and homemade fruit pie.

Then, when Joel was in third grade, his mother was in the accident which left her back broken, requiring traction and long-term hospitalization. This misfortune coincided with the traditional third grade increase in homework, the change from "learning to read" to "reading to learn," and the introduction of inference into reading comprehension. By nature, Joel is a concrete thinker who has trouble with abstractions.

In the middle of the school year, each child was asked to do a long-term reading assignment and written report on an explorer. Joel was excited at first, but he didn't know how to read the long words. Then, he lost his book, fell behind, and didn't keep track of when the report was due. He was also having increasing difficulty listening in class.

He was worrying about his mother. This lowered his concentration, which, in turn, raised a high level of anxiety. He wondered why he wasn't doing better and what was wrong with him. He was trying as hard as he could, but not getting much success.

When he tried to start writing the report, his hand tired easily from his cramped handwriting. He tried to include some of the big words from the book, but he didn't understand them. He didn't know where to begin or how to get going. His teacher didn't help him out, because — since he wasn't a disciplinary problem — he hadn't attracted attention, and she didn't have any idea how deep a hole he was getting into.

When the medical re-evaluation indicated his mother would require extended hospitalization, his aunt — a teacher in a nearby school system — volunteered to leave her own family four nights a week to come and stay at Joel's house. Because she was on a tight schedule herself, and because it was her nature, she established regular hours for everyone. She posted a large calendar, so everyone would know everyone else's plans and obligations. She carved out a homework area — not just for the boys, she needed one, too. She helped Joel make an organizational grid for his report using the 6 *wh* words. All together, the family decided on a daily checklist which they posted on the fridge. They promised themselves the reward of a movie every week each person's checklist was complete.

With these supportive structures in place, Joel's academics improved, his anxiety diminished, and his concentration returned. The summer plan is for him to take a "Kids and Computers" course. He will learn keyboard fingering and word processing, and the family will get a computer which his father will use, too. His father may be able to do some of his work at home with this electronic aid, and therefore spend more time with the boys.

These structures hadn't seemed vital when the kids were young, when Mom was at home, and when Dad's job was secure. But, this isn't the 1950's. When uncertainties, dislocations, and variables entered the picture, there was no shell for the egg, and no skeletal structure on which to hang needs and plans. Joel's mother's broken back seemed symbolic of what was happening to the whole family. Now, full recovery is under way, with the bones predicted to be stronger than before the breaks.

Chapter EIGHT

CHILDREN WHO SEEM LIKE CHANGELINGS

Swans and Ducklings

From folklore to Gilbert and Sullivan, not to mention soap operas, the changeling child deviates from the expected. Stolen by fairies who leave a substitute infant, switched at birth for one another, or put under a spell by witchcraft, they set adults on their ears and make hash of the status quo.

Sometimes, changelings are dark when the others in the family are fair. Sometimes, as in *H.M.S. Pinafore*, they stubbornly fall in love out of their social and economic station, pitting tender romance against hard worldly dictates, until the secret of their true identity is revealed. Sometimes, their stories amuse and warm the reader, as in Mark Twain's *A Connecticut Yankee In King Arthur's Court*. Other times, they chill the reader's soul with fear, when — under their childish beauty — they embody evil, as in Henry James' masterpiece, *The Turn of the Screw*. Changelings' stories draw power from this fact: they are different. The same is true for some real live kids and their families.

Probably, each of us can think of a family in which parents and one or more of their offspring don't have that "goodness of fit" which makes life proceed smoothly.

Most parents don't realize the rigidity of the mold they've constructed, until a child comes along who doesn't fit. They may not even be aware that such a mold exists. A child who resembles the parents fits the contours comfortably and is thought to be "easy" or "good;" the child who is different may seem "difficult" or "bad."

It doesn't matter where the difference lies. The musical parents whose child is a tone-deaf sports fiend are perplexed. So, too, in all likelihood, are the extroverts who produce a loner, the verbal eggheads who produce a hands-on engineer, or the traditionalists who produce an artist. Particularly if they take their parenting seriously, they may ask themselves, "What's wrong?", "What shall we do?", or, as if this is a child of a rogue gene — a swan among the ducklings — "Where DID this kid come from?"

Difference provokes conflict. Conflict generates anger, resistance, discouragement, frustration, sadness, or reluctance, leaving parents perplexed and the child feeling rebellious, rejected, abandoned, or unlovable and unloved.

We know the corrosive effect of negative emotions on living, on relationships with oneself and others, and on learning. The downward spiral of emotional habit; personal frustration; and difficulty acquiring new skills, information, and concepts in a changeling child is predictable, but also preventable.

School is the parents' first chance to see how their child fares when out from under the protective wing, and they often equate early academic performance with a crystal ball view of success or failure in later life. Therefore, if learning patterns deviate from family expectations, pressures intensify as adults try to force the child to conform.

Healthy children will stubbornly try to protect themselves with the weapons at their command: resistance, refusal, rebellion. Children who feel powerless may go underground, resorting to subterfuge or turning their anger inward, risking genuine depression. Misunderstanding leads to hurt, which in turn creates pressure, angry words, or retreat from communication.

Does this only happen to bad people? No. Eight-year-old Arnold and his mother came in to my office tired out from trying to get along with one another: a horse-and-buggy mother with a tractor-trailer kid.

Their latest confrontation had erupted over Arnold's birthday cake. Thinking this time she'd be able to help him have a good time in the kitchen, Libby had promised Arnold he could frost the cake. She showed him how, he gave a couple of swipes with the spatula, but then some chocolate crumbs got into the white frosting, and, in frustration, he shifted gears. "Batter up," he called out, whereupon he held the spatula like a baseball bat, threw a dollop of frosting in the air, and gave it a Babe Ruth-sized smack. Libby cried, "Stop. No, Arnold." He tossed another dollop and took another swing. She snatched the spatula and hit him with it across the back of hand. She started to cry. He started to howl. His father came in, saying, "What's going on?" Libby said,"He's a terrible child." Arnold threw the cake plate on the floor and ran away to his room.

For Libby, Arnold is a foreign country; she misunderstands the language, her pockets hold no currency, she has no visa, she cannot find her way along the highways and byways, and she doesn't catch on to the signals being broadcast.

Arnold feels like an expatriate in his own house. He hears his mother and father say kind words to him, but their body English shows confusion, irritation, exasperation, and even dislike.

Feeling estranged from the adult world, he brings with him into the classroom emotional habits of mistrust, confusion, defensiveness, and resentment. Arnold has trouble working not only with his teachers, but also with peers. His grades suffer, his eagerness to learn is dampened, and neither he nor his parents can take pride in his performance.

Are parents who get caught in such a struggle unworthy, uncaring, unfeeling? By no means. Usually, they are worrying over the incompatibility, doubting themselves, and (as they grow more tense and fearful) desperately clinging to their own ways, in hopes of making things come out right or "turning the kid around."

In such swan-and-duckling instances, with misplaced determination on one hand and misinterpreted stubbornness on the other, misunderstandings multiply, communication falters, and affection lies fallow. Yet, both sides are lonely; each is afraid.

Frustration, irritation, or — yes, we need to admit it — dislike wear down parental patience, and spend emotional energies which would otherwise be available for pride and encouragement. As we have seen in many instances throughout the book, anger is often the product of guilt and fear. Children who seem like changelings are extremely vulnerable. Why?

Kids, even rebellious ones, look to their parents for deep personal values. While they may wear green hair or Doc Marten boots with party clothes to conform to current fashion, underneath they absorb their parents' guiding moral/ethical codes. When kids see themselves as deeply at variance with what their parents profoundly believe and want, they must question whether they themselves are fundamentally flawed. Mistrust of oneself and questions of one's own worth devour energy as they destroy self-concept.

What happens to kids who want to love their parents, who also want to love themselves, and who think they aren't all that bad? There are only three ways to reconcile opposition: one side or the other must change, or give up, or be destroyed. We see some children whose healthy stubbornness keeps them fighting on their own behalf. They can only win the battle by annihilating the parental codes and voices they carry inside. Such metaphoric patricide or matricide, which may be necessary for the survival of an individual spirit, brings both terror and guilt in its execution. A veritable conflagration of conflict ensues, scorching the souls of those engaged in would-be loving but deadly combat for control.

And, far apart as the two sides stand, they are alike in their emotional stances and habits: fear where there should be trust, despair where there should be hope, acrimony in place of affection, conflict in place of harmony, and guilt instead of pride.

When parents and kids who are caught in these emotional patterns meet the outside world of employment or school, they bring their baggage with them with predictable results, as we saw in Arnold's case.

Children who have the double misfortune of being different from their parents and also from their teacher must either disengage their emotional and intellectual gears, abandon themselves as they try to be reborn in someone else's image, or fight for their own psychological and conceptual lives.

Because the destructive power of these situations is so obvious, and because the unleashed negative forces tie so strongly to the feelings and situations we have explored in earlier parts of the book, we need to ask ourselves if such differences must always bring distress?

If we cast our thoughts to the concept of discrepancy rather than disobedience, much of the conflict may dissolve.

We, as adults, need to give ourselves the gift of four metaphoric "sockets." If we — and the children in our care — plug into them, we can release and channel benevolent circuits of emotional energy and conceptual power.

Four Sockets

1. We need to raise our consciousness that situations of "badness of fit" can exist among decent, loving, intelligent people. The difference is no one's fault. How the difference is addressed is everyone's opportunity.

We will see specific tips and strategies in the next few pages.

2. In looking for desirable or undesirable traits, and impressive or mediocre thinking, we need to move beyond previous restrictive definitions, expanding our thinking to include the works of Howard Gardner, Robert Sternberg, Alan Kaufman, Joseph Renzulli, Albert Galaburda, and my own work on the education of the gifted. Familiarity with these works gives us additional lenses through which to see and help students, not to mention one another.

⊕ *In Frames of Mind: the Theory of Multiple Intelligences*, Howard Gardner describes seven separate intelligences: logical/mathematical, linguistic, spatial, musical, bodily/kinesthetic, interpersonal, and intrapersonal.

Evident as these abilities are in many major thinkers and contributors to our civilization, they may not raise a student's grade point average, and many of these intelligences go hand-in-hand with school failure. Gardner provides a scientifically respected way of seeing where a child is "at promise" as well as at "at risk." Drawing from anthropology and the arts, as well as from education and science, he offers a generous way of looking at human beings.

Gardner's work provides an expanded view of intelligence and giftedness. It is inclusive, innovative, and judged scientifically sound by his peers in medicine, science, and education.

Since there is no normed test for these intelligences at this time, short-cut seekers will be disappointed. But, those who enjoy being sensitive observer/diagnosticians will be rewarded by clearer vision. The Six Specific Activities for Teachers in this chapter are built around Gardner's intelligences.

⊕ In his book, *Beyond I.Q.: A Triarchic Theory of Human Intelligence*, Robert J. Sternberg teases apart three aspects of intelligence, and then shows us how each human being weaves them back together into a personal intelligence. He asks us to look at:

internal intelligence - what the child or adult brings from within

external intelligence - what the child or adult absorbs from the outside

internal and external intelligence combined - the unique way each person fuses the two into perception, concepts, and ways of meeting and coping with life situations

Sternberg believes that giftedness shows in superior skill in insight and the ability to deal with novelty, and also allows for the inclusion of common sense and "street smarts" in measuring intelligence, increasing the opportunities and ways a person may show as intelligent. Thus, his bias is towards inclusion. His interpretation of both giftedness and learning disabilities implies that some people will fit both categories at once.

⊕ Alan and Nadine Kaufman's work, based on the work of the Russian neurologist A.R.Luria, and on the Kaufmans' experiences working with David Wechsler on the development of his intelligence tests, distinguishes between *simultaneous* and *sequential* thinking and learning.

The Kaufmans add a heretofore missing dimension to the evaluation and discussion of an individual's learning style. The spontaneous, intuitive learner may do poorly in a bottom-to-top, sequentially organized curriculum. The child with weak rote memory who prefers manipulatives to symbols may have severe academic problems, and be very intelligent. Discrepant patterns are confusing until we see their origins.

⊕ Galaburda, continuing the work of Geschwind, shows us that tremendous potential for such *3-dimensional* areas as engineering, mathematics, science, medicine, the arts, athletics, drama, politics or the ability to fix the family car can coexist with difficulty in the *2-dimensional* areas of reading writing, spelling, or pencil-paper arithmetic.

When kids do well on the athletic field but have poor handwriting, when an accomplished math student is a halting, clumsy reader, or when an artist can see the spaces in a building but not the spaces between letters in a spelling word, the adult world often loses patience, saying, "You only learn what you feel like learning." This unfair, negative judgement undermines students' trust in their own powers and enjoyment of their own talents. Such students need multi-sensory methods and materials, and opportunities to display their considerable skills.

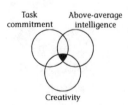

Task commitment

Above-average intelligence

Creativity

⊕ Renzulli, in his work on the recognition and nurture of giftedness, uses this overlapping circles model. We see that he refers to above-average intelligence, avoiding stratospherically high cut-off numbers. He speaks of task commitment, which is psychological and intellectual availability for learning, focus, and willingness to risk. He refers to creativity, for which it is our job to provide stimulus and showcase. This model, like the preceding ones, is inclusive rather than exclusive, permits many different combinations of talents and outcomes, and helps us recognize gifts and talents which may not have been apparent.

⊕ In my own work on the recognition and education of the gifted, I have found ten traits which frequently cluster together in gifted people. These move us beyond the idea that intelligence is verifiable in any one single test score. They are: *recognition of new material, awareness of patterns, energy* (psychological and emotional as well as physical), *curiosity, drive and concentration,* wide and deep *experiential and emotional memory* which may or may not accompany strong rote memory, *empathy, heightened perceptions, invulnerability* in the area of particular talent, and *divergent thinking.*

While these traits are exhilarating, they can also bring pain and misunderstanding. Knowing that different learners disrupt traditional classrooms, parents and teachers who are aware of these traits can see originality and creativity for what they truly are.

3. We need to create a "proclivities profile" on ourselves and on each kid in our family or classroom. It needn't be a polished literary document; something as simple as a piece of fool's cap, with a line drawn down the middle and columns headed + and -, will do nicely. Jot on it those things the person seeks out and those things the person avoids. Plan accordingly.

4. We need to share this proclivities profile with each child. Respond to their feedback by making alterations or additions. Support weaknesses, nurture talent.

The above show us many ways for intelligent, well-intentioned people to think differently, and to walk on divergent paths. That's what this chapter is all about. And, that is why this chapter makes a fitting conclusion to the book.

Emotion is the On/Off switch for learning. When we understand each other, we can create those opportunities for original expression which foster confidence and which — through their diversity — can bring delight and discovery to our culture. When differences are denied, or control becomes a reason for battle, negative emotions weaken the generator and interrupt the flow of energy from the power plant, leaving pockets of untapped power and unlighted reservoirs of imagination.

Because the story of Adam and his family, One Child's Story, illuminates this kind of situation with so many shards and prisms, it carries the weight of this chapter. The other sections, consistent with the organization of the rest of the book, are foreshortened.

Ten Tips for Moms, Dads, Nannies, Grannies, Grandfathers, Teachers, and Other Concerned Adults

1. Expand our own notions of what is worthwhile, seeing how thinking works in different ways, finding many ways of measuring success, and remembering the inclusionists cited above.

2. Identify specific strengths and encourage interests. Particularly when adult and child talents and interest differ, it is the adults who must take the initiative in dignifying what the child cares about. Otherwise, the child infers that the interest is either shameful or sub-standard, or decides to hide it from the world. Beware. Unexercised talents itch.

Individual passions form the complexity, character, and texture of a person's whole life. And, interests must be encouraged if they are to grow. They can't simply be put in the freezer to be thawed out in adulthood.

3. Support weaknesses. Each of us has weaknesses. When a child's strengths differ from those of the adults in his or her world, the weaknesses may show as glaring flaws. Unsupported weaknesses ache.

4. Accept differences. Sounds obvious. Sounds easy. In conversation, reading, or rehashing the evening news, point out how people differ from one another, as well as how they are alike. See the potential interest, flint, and humor in situations which combine different talents. Give each other space. The family needn't march everywhere together like a military unit. When interests collide or tastes grate, separation can lessen irritation.

5. Hold on and let go:

hold fast to a common set of human values

avoid living vicariously through children

maintain personal adult interests

6. Carve out separate territories for siblings. Children need individual arenas.

7. Banish adult arrogance (or guilt) in assuming responsibility for a child's innate ways. Children deserve ownership of who they are. Their own pride of accomplishment must not belong to someone else who is "responsible" for their makeup.

8. Offer time.

9. Listen as well as talk

10. Cherish humor

These ten principles open the way to relaxation, enjoyment, and mutual respect.

Six Specific Activities for Teachers

These are consistent with the priorities laid out in the first chapter, and also offer an activity to exercise or tap each of Gardner's intelligences.

1. Logical/mathematical

Patternmaster. Recognizing, identifying, manipulating, changing, and reconstructing patterns is a hallmark of logical/mathematical intelligence. Even preschool children can play in this domain. Start simply. A long lace and some colored wooden beads for threading will do the trick. Perhaps the adult will string six beads: blue, red, blue, red, blue, red. What color comes next?

Then, try a pattern of threes: red, black, yellow, red, black, yellow. What color comes next?

For an older child, the adult might explain that colors combine to make other shades: red and blue make purple, blue and yellow make green. If I string red-purple-blue, yellow-green-blue, what color bead should come in the middle of this string: red-?-white?

Number patterns provide endless entertainment. What's the missing number: 2,4,8,16, ? What comes next: 1,4,7,10, ?

As soon as the child is comfortable with patterns others have made, ask him or her to invent patterns for others to decipher.

2. Linguistic

Journals. Children with linguistic talent — or those who need to develop stronger linguistic muscles — profit from recording their thoughts, experiences, questions, and emotions. Should journals be private? Are they fair game for a teacher to read? To show to a parent? One teacher solved this ethical dilemma by designating one-day-a-week's entry for adult eyes, the other days to be private unless the writer chose to share.

3. Spatial

Chess and 3-D Tic-Tac-Toe. These are ideal ways for children to flex or strengthen their spatial conceptual muscles. Both games should be in the classroom with time set aside before the official start of the day, or at some time during the day for kids to play. Ideally, several (leading to many) will get interested. A classroom or inter-grade league is exciting for all.

4. Musical.

Listen and respond. Some very musical children may not know how to play an instrument. But, all children can listen. The teacher should designate a time — such as Thursdays after recess, or Tuesday during lunch, or Monday morning for the first five minutes of the school day — and should play a piece of music on a cassette or CD. The children should just listen the first time. The second time, they should respond by drawing representational figures, or simply by putting pieces of color together. The purpose is to have an individual aesthetic response to something the whole group has heard together. Then, share and compare. Obviously, there is no right or wrong answer. Exercises such as this, which honor originality over conformity, encourage individuality.

5. Bodily/kinesthetic

Act Up. Write out actions to be pantomimed on index cards. Put the index cards in a bag. Let each child reach in, pull out a card, act out the situation, and see if the rest of kids can tell what is happening. Here are five suggestions:

It is a very hot summer day. Order, pay for, and receive an ice cream cone. Eat it without dribbling or without dropping the ice cream ball on the sidewalk.

Take off your coat. Get out the sewing kit. Choose a button. Sew it on.

Go into the kitchen. Get out some bread and dig around in the refrigerator for cheese, meat, lettuce, etc. Make a sandwich. Eat it.

Wake up. Get out of bed. Brush your teeth. Get dressed. Can your classmates tell what you chose to put on?

Pretend you are Marcel Marceau, the famous mime. Open the door to an imaginary box. Step in and close the door behind you. Begin to see the walls pressing down and in on you. Try to hold them away. Find the door again and escape.

6. Personal Intelligences: Interpersonal, Intrapersonal

Pick a Partner. Let each student select a person from history, the arts, athletics, or politics. Read to find out the good and bad things about this person. Decide why you chose this person. Decide what attributes drew the person into their field.

Then, pair the students up. Ask them to pretend to be their character. Staying in character, talk to their partner. Do they get along? What questions would they ask each other? What would they admire in each other? What would they dislike? After they separate, ask each to write a letter to the other saying what they enjoyed about the meeting. Would they like to meet again? Why?

Empathy — and the ability to sit in someone else's skin — exercise and expand both interpersonal and intrapersonal intelligences.

ONE CHILD'S STORY
"I'm Not You, I'm Me"

"Adam, put down that toy and listen to me. I want you to pay attention."

"I am paying attention."

"Nine is too old for this kind of behavior. You've lost your homework again, and you still haven't learned that multiplication table. What's going on with you? You don't do anything worthwhile."

"I'm half-way finished making this model."

"Model! That's just what I'm talking about. Models are toys, Adam. What about real things? You spend your time gluing pieces of plastic together upstairs in your room...making toys out of toys. You can't even handle simple responsibilities like feeding the dog."

"I fed the dog."

"But, not when you were supposed to."

"But, I fed her."

"Stop talking back to me."

"I only said I fed the dog."

"You have to learn to do things on schedule, so people can depend on you."

"Dad, I just told you. I fed the dog."

"You're not listening to me."

"You're the one who's not listening."

"No allowance if you're rude."

"But, Dad, I need that allowance for my next model."

"Next model? You've probably spent the money before you've even gotten it! When your brother was 9, he started a stamp collection. Today, it's worth something, and Jeff's doing well."

"Well, I'm not Jeff. I'm me."

"You're a dreamer, Adam, and dreamers get crushed in the real world."

"You don't mean that, Walt. You're a dreamer, too, in your own way."

"But, I'm also a realist, Janet. You know as well as I do that you've got to start good habits early, if you're ever going to amount to anything: being on time, paying attention, getting your school-work done. Work first, play later. In this family, we get things done."

Adam's voice quavered. "I thought families were supposed to be made up of people. This family just seems like a bunch of rules and good report cards."

"That's not fair, Adam."

"Oh, yes, it is, Janet. That's what we need a little more of from this particular family member. Hand me that model, Adam."

"Why? Dad. Please."

"I said give me the model."

"Don't, Dad."

"I'm not going to do anything to it. I'm just going to lock it in my desk drawer until you memorize the 7's table, and do your house-hold help jobs."

"But, the glue isn't dry. It'll..."

"Here, Adam, I know a good place for it. I'll put it away."

Walt reached out to take the model from one side, Janet from the other, and the pieces came apart in their hands.

"I'm sorry. I didn't mean..."

"You broke it. You broke my model on purpose."

"...for your own good."

Adam ran upstairs.

"I don't know what's happening to this family, but I don't like it."

"We've never shouted at each other like that before. I don't understand. You're not yourself when you speak to him that way. I know you love him, but you sounded so hard."

"Sure, I love him, but somebody's got to be hard... somebody's got to make him see."

"I'm not sure hard is right. He's not like Jeff. Jeff was always organized and fell right in with our way of doing things. Adam is different."

"I think he's being different on purpose. Disorganized. Stubborn. He's always been stubborn, and I think he's lazy, too."

"I feel terrible about his model. What are we going to do?"

"Just what I said. The pieces are staying in my drawer until he's done as he's been told. He needs to know who's calling the shots."

"Calling the shots? That sounds like warfare. This is a 9-year-old boy!"

"A 9-year-old boy who's challenging us, his teachers, practically the whole adult world."

"You take everything too personally, Walt. Maybe it's not challenge. Maybe he's just doing things his own way."

"If his own way is what we've been seeing, it's got to change. You don't like it any more than I do. Admit it, Janet. I heard you talking on the phone to your sister yesterday, saying just what I'm saying. Why do you say it to your sister but not to me?"

"I can talk to my sister, and she doesn't yell at me."

"Oh, great! Go talk to *her* then..."

As a baby, Adam had been healthy, alert, and unusually responsive to color and shape. When he learned to walk, he was curious about his surroundings, very loving, and at the same time, had a decided independent streak.

"I remember when we went off for a long weekend to celebrate our fifth wedding anniversary. Your mother kept the kids. She said they were angels. But, when we got back, Adam wouldn't make eye contact with me for two days. I was really upset. Then, finally he forgot or forgave, I don't know which, and everything was OK again."

"Remember how he was about food? Before he was even one-year-old, he insisted on feeding himself. If you or I tried, he'd push the spoon away or clamp his mouth shut at the last minute. If we let him pick the food up in his fingers, he was as content as any kid you'd hope to find. Later on, he figured out a pretty good spoon routine all on his own."

"He was just as independent about the bike. I remember how he watched the kid next door riding back and forth on his little, purple two-wheeler. When we got him the red bike as a surprise, I tried to teach him how to ride it, but he resisted. For a while, I thought he just didn't want to learn from me, and my feelings were hurt.

"Then, one day, when the other kid left his purple bike outside, Adam stood it up, got on, and rode away. I realized he hadn't wanted to learn from being told; he wanted to figure it out himself from watching. After that, he was on his own red bike all the time. He learned to whistle that same year. I can see him now — so happy — riding and whistling."

First Grade: "He fiddles with toys instead of listening."

"Both of us are logical and systematic," Walt said to the first grade teacher at the fall conference. "Janet's a librarian, and the work I do at the company warehouse...well, if I wasn't really organized, I'd be fired. At home, we're trying to help Adam be more focused and orderly, but it's hard."

"Adam has a hard time settling in to work," said his teacher. "He keeps a Lego inside his desk no matter how many times I ask him to put it in his cubby. And, when I'm explaining something, he's usually fiddling with toys or paper clips and rubber bands. He has trouble recognizing sight words, and his mistakes distort meaning. Yesterday, he read button for banana, and I can tell you that took the logic out of the passage about monkeys!"

Summer Arts Program: "Follow the directions."

"Adam needs to learn how to wait and to listen," said his counselor at the summer arts program. "On our dinosaur dioramas, he made the best shoe-box model in the class, but on our astronomy project, he was too impatient to read the directions on folding the paper to make the planet models. When I saw he had it wrong, I tried to explain what he should do differently, but he lost his temper, crumpled his up, and threw it away."

Third Grade: "Maybe he forgets, maybe he just isn't trying."

"Third grade math is hard for some children," explained Adam's teacher on parents' night. "We work with pencil and paper more than with manipulatives. I require my students to memorize their multiplication tables by mid-year. We play Round the World for drill, and children who don't memorize easily have a hard time. Third grade is also the year for polishing handwriting and tackling those spelling demons. I give plenty of extra help to children who are trying, but I'm tough on the lazy ones. It's the right time to tighten up."

Later, Walt said, "That teacher may be just what Adam needs, or he might be in for boot camp. He loves numbers and measuring, but memorizing is different. Maybe he just forgets, maybe he isn't trying. I don't know."

"I'm worried, too. Memorizing math facts will be hard enough, but throwing in a lot of spelling demons...I still feel sick about that fight, when we broke his model."

"We didn't break it, it was an accident. Even Adam understands that now. But, we've got to figure out a way to make him buckle down."

"What about getting him a computer for his birthday? It's early enough in the year that he'll be able to use it for his schoolwork. I know he said he wanted karate lessons, but this will be better in the long run. We can get him some math games, I know there must be some spelling programs, and a machine could take some of the pressure off his handwriting."

"He's always liked doing things with his hands... What a great idea! It will be a total surprise. Thank heavens we finally agree on something about Adam. Usually, when we talk about him, we fight."

Fourth Grade: "But he's just not using his mind."

"We're confused and upset," Adam's parents said to his fourth grade teacher. "We want him to do well in school, but we don't seem to be getting very far. Last year, we bought him a computer for his birthday. Even though it was a big investment, we thought he could use it to get more organized, to memorize his math and spelling, and for doing some story-writing.

"We both came home early from work on his birthday and set up the components on a special table in the corner of his room, so it would be all ready and waiting when he got home. We kept every one of the packing boxes, in case some part didn't work. He was polite enough, but his face just fell. We took turns showing him how to work the spelling and math games, and he tried a couple of times while we were sitting there with him. After his birthday supper, he went right up to his room, and he was there for a long time. We said to each other 'It's working!' But, that wasn't what we saw when we went upstairs to put him to bed.

"He had spread the packing boxes around on the floor. Then, he had taken out his collection of things like paper towel rollers, odd bits of wire, old switches...just a lot of junk. He was fitting bits and pieces onto the cartons, covering some of them with aluminum foil. He said he was making a space station.

"That space station covered his floor the whole winter. Every night, he'd go up and fiddle with it. He turned his set of little rubber men into colonists, and made up a whole series of adventures about them. Another boy used to come and play space station with him. They invented a space language, space food, even space sports. The computer gathered dust; it was the most expensive paper weight in town.

"Adam muddled through his schoolwork last year, but he still trips up on 7 x 8, and he doesn't remember whether friend is spelled *ei* or *ie*. We think he's bright enough, but he's just not using his mind."

Interlude

"Hey, Adam, how come you're going away to summer camp?"

"My parents say it was good for my brother."

Fifth Grade: "They can't make me."

"My teachers only tell me all the things I do wrong. I have good ideas, but they want me to do everything their way, and they act like there's only one way. Well, it's not my way, and they can't make me."

"Adam, be reasonable."

"You're just like them! You keep trying to make me act like you, and be like you. Well, I'm not you. I'm me!"

"Lower your voice, and stop being rude!"

"I've done a lot of good things at school they never even noticed. Who do they think fixed the pump for the aquarium? Who stopped Steve and Fred from picking on that little kid in the locker room? They think I'm bad? I'll show them bad...and you, too!"

* * *

"Mr. and Mrs. Martin, I'm sorry to say that Adam has slid consistently down hill since we met in September. He is failing, and his attitude is getting worse. As his home room teacher, I want to go over some comments with you:

Math: Adam is intuitive but rebellious. He gets the right answers to his problems but refuses to record his process on paper. He has a better sense of space and dimension than any student I have ever taught, but until he supports his good guess work with conventional methods, he will not have the tools for higher math at which he ought to excel.

English: Adam's writing is original but extremely disorganized. He fails many comprehension exercises because he argues with the teachers about which ideas are of major importance. Disorganization and stubbornness are a dangerous combination, and now he is also becoming disruptive in class. He broke the class up the other day, saying, 'Hey, you guys, did you know that weird and wired have the same letters. Which do you want to be?' He stuck two fingers in a pretend light socket, and waved the fingers of the other hand in the air over his head, as if his hair was standing on end from electric shock, saying, 'Weird, man...I'm wired!'

Science: The balloon caper was not funny and has cost Adam a failing grade for this six-week period."

The Birthday Party: "...such an elaborate present!"

"I've never had a nicer birthday. What a lucky grandmother I am, and what a wonderful family. Janet and Walt, that light-weight wheelbarrow is exactly the one I've been looking at in the gardening catalogue. Jeff, I can count on you to keep me up to date on music. I'll listen to your tape in the car, and I'll play it on my Walkman when I'm mucking around in the garden. And, I still have a present left to open from Adam. I always look forward to your presents; you make such wonderful things.

"Why, Adam, cologne AND powder...I figured the fancy box was just borrowed from your mother. I...my goodness, Adam, such an elaborate present, why...thank you. Thank you all so much."

* * *

"Adam, sit up here in the front seat. I want to talk to you. I want to know about that birthday present. That wasn't like you at all.

Where did it come from?"

"She liked it, didn't she? What's the big deal?"

"Liked it? Yes, she liked it, but I think she was kind of disappointed it wasn't something you made."

"Last year, you were mean about my present. You told me you didn't know what she'd ever do with it. You said it was just pieces of wood junked up together."

"Oh, Adam, we straightened that mistake out right then. It was a misunderstanding. Please. Let's not go back over that again."

"I wasn't the one who brought it up. You did," said Adam. "Nothing I do is right. If I make a funny present, you say I'm too old for baby stuff. Now, I buy one, that's no good either, and you're on my case again."

"Adam, where DID you get the money to pay for that set? Those things are expensive."

"I had it."

"Where did you get it?"

"It was mine. I just had it."

"You never have extra money. That's one of the things you can't seem to learn: handling your allowance and finding ways to earn."

"I had it. I tell you I had it. Why are you accusing me?"

"I'm not accusing. I'm asking. And, I don't think you're telling the truth. Where did you get that money, Adam?"

"This car's too hot. I need some air."

"Close the window, Adam, and answer me. Now."

"Please, Walt. This isn't right. Let's wait till we get home."

"Now!"

"I lent it to him, Dad," Jeff interjected, just as Adam was blurting out, "I...I found it."

"Jeff says he lent it, you say you found it, I say you took it."

"Stop! That's not true. Our child doesn't steal. Adam has never taken anything in his whole life!"

"Adam didn't 'have' that money, and he didn't 'find' it. He found a way to 'FIND' it, call it whatever you want."

"I'll pay it back. I promise I'll pay it back. For once, I wanted to do the BEST thing in this family. Every other time, the grown-ups and Jeff are perfect, and then there's me. You think I don't try. You think I don't care. You're wrong. But, everything I do just makes things worse. I wish I'd never been born!"

Fear: "It's not doing any good."

"It's a terrible thing to realize you're giving up on your own kid, but I admit that's how I feel."

"I'm angry and worried. I'm frustrated and I'm confused. I find myself coming down hard on Adam all the time. I don't like it, and it's not doing any good. The bad things are getting worse, and the good things are disappearing. In a way, I've seen this coming for a long time. In a way, it's a collection of bad surprises. A lot of things bother me...this is a kid I love...or try to. This is the kid who used to be happy; he used to whistle."

A Helping Hand: "I have some ideas about Adam."

"As a guidance counselor, I'm particularly interested in sixth graders. It's our last shot before adolescence. In looking through some student records, I spotted Adam. He reminds me of myself at that age, and I have some ideas."

"I'm glad YOU do."

"First of all, he needs a piece of success. I don't care how small or how inconsequential it seems to the rest of us, but it should be something Adam cares about. We have to catch him in the act...of doing something well. Then, we can find a way to weave that success into his school life. We have to help him show his talented and cooperative side to his teachers and his peers, not to mention to himself.

"Second, Adam's whole style of learning and thinking may be different from yours. Differences in approach can be mistaken for no approach at all, or for bad habits. Some kids (and grown-ups) learn very quickly when they see demonstrations or can move concrete objects around with their hands, but they have trouble with long verbal or written explanations. Adam sounds like that to me.

"Some people — kids or adults — are systematic learners. They like to go from part to whole, collecting bits of information and building them sequentially into a concept. Other bright kids learn the opposite way. They need to start with the big idea, and move from the whole down to the parts. Whether we talk about part-to-whole/whole-to-part, or bottom-to-top/top-to-bottom learning, it's the same distinction. I need to begin with whole-to-part myself, and from Adam's report cards, comments, and history, I suspect he does, too. This learning style is a mismatch for the way many textbook writers work, and many teachers teach.

"Different styles go hand in hand with different preferences — for activities, interests, or life's work. Not better, not worse, just different. Remember, variety is healthy."

"What would you like US to do?" Janet asked.

"Nothing, right now. I know it's still August, and school hasn't started yet, but I think it's time to hear from Adam himself. A sixth grader is old enough to have a hand in his own planning. I'd like to talk to him, probably several times. Then, we'll get back together."

Reaching Out: "My whole life is being in trouble."

"I don't get it, Mr. Tripp." Adam was suspicious. "You're asking ME what kinds of things I like to do. People don't ask kids that; they tell 'em. 'Specially kids like me."

* * *

"OK, Mr. Tripp, here's the list. I don't know if it's what you meant, but I wrote down a bunch of things I did that were fun. Most of them weren't from school, and the things that were fun in school aren't what I would write down for a teacher. About my favorite, I think it was that space station I built in third grade. I was just a little kid, but it was great.

"I used the big cardboard cartons my computer came in and the molded styrofoam packing. I thought it looked like something from space. I set up buildings and domes with connectors and launch pads. I made secret tunnels with the tubes from paper towel rolls. Me and my friend took a whole bunch of little rubber guys and made them into the aliens who lived there. We printed special money for them. We used Lego motors from when we were younger and made space machines with moving parts. We turned an old walkie-talkie set into a broadcasting station, and we used little silver film cans for defense rockets. My parents thought it was just dumb fooling around, and my mom was mad because she couldn't clean my room. I guess I should have felt guilty about not using the computer much, but my space colony was more interesting."

* * *

"OK, Mr. Tripp. Here's the next list. I did what you said. Here are the things I really don't like.

"In math, I like the ideas. They make sense, so I get the answers fast. I just know I'm right, and it's stupid to have to sit there and write it all down when I've already done it in my head. It's like having to write down a conversation after you've finished talking.

"I don't like to memorize. Spelling is BORING!

"In social studies, I like finding out about what different people do. I even like geography. But, the teacher doesn't let us do anything. We just sit there, and he talks. I hate having to sit and listen all the time. I stop paying attention, I get thinking about something more interesting, and then I get caught when he asks me a question.

"Sometimes, I just feel like saying something funny. I always know how to crack the other kids up. Sometimes, I do things they wouldn't dare, and then I'm in trouble again.

"And, I guess that's the truth of it right there. My whole life is being in trouble. The teachers are down on my case. So are my parents. Nothing I do seems right. Even my name...Adam. What am I? On trial for original sin?"

Connections: "There isn't even a clover leaf."

"Adam, you're intelligent and honest. We're going to help you turn things around. This year, we've sectioned you with some teachers you'll get along with. In social studies, you'll have a series of projects along with the reading. In English, your teacher is in touch with the local newspaper, and I bet you'll be published by June. Your math teacher is good at deciding when it's important to write out the steps, and when it doesn't matter. We're also going to have a math lab. We may ask you to help some of the younger kids. You have lots of energy, and we need you.

"You're going to find school a lot more to your liking. But, you have to take responsibility too: handing in assignments on time, behavior in class. You're too smart for me to have to outline them for you.

"One more thing. Our school is planning a PTA fundraising fair. Mrs. Debeny is writing a play with parts for kids in every grade. They need volunteers. You and your parents might like to help out."

"I don't know about that last part, Mr. Tripp. Whenever my parents and I try to do anything together, we end up in a fight. It's as if they're a car on one highway going one direction, I'm a car heading a different way on a different road, and there isn't even a cloverleaf."

A Different View: "We'll make a Propensities Report."

"You've got a great kid here."

"Great kid? He's in trouble right here in your school. We fight at home, and there was even a terrible episode over his grandmother's birthday."

"I know, he told me about it."

"And, you still say he's a great kid?"

"Yes. Of course, it's wrong to take money. But, he won't do that again. Look what he was trying to do — please you by doing things your way."

"Now, look here, stealing's not our way."

"Of course not. And, it isn't Adam's, either. He felt cornered, so he did something wrong. Adam is a sensitive, very intelligent boy. Underneath his bravado and shenanigans, he wants to be in touch with his own good qualities, but he doesn't want to sell out to a world he thinks is trying to make him be something or someone he's not. It takes a lot of strength and courage to do what Adam is doing; in a way, he's fighting for his life."

"But, look where it's getting him. Deeper and deeper into a hole!"

"Yes, right now that's true. He's misguided and uncomfortable with himself. That's where we need to help him."

"How?"

"I'm going to ask you to do the same thing I asked Adam to do. Both of you — separately — make a list of Adam's good points, strengths, and talents. Put down the things he likes to do, things he does well, things that make his eyes light up. And, by the way, I'd put independence and stubbornness in the plus column. Then, make a list of things he dislikes and does poorly. Then, combine your lists.

We're going to make a Propensities Report, and I think the patterns will be very clear."

* * *

"I agree completely. You say Adam is artistic, articulate, creative, good company for himself, sensitive, humorous, intuitive, honest, kind, generous, stubborn, and brave. You say he enjoys building and making things, he can stick to a task (of his own choosing), and he can concentrate for a long time. By nature, he is more of a whole-to-part than part-to-whole learner, he prefers demonstrations to explanations, and he enjoys working with other people.

"You both see him as weak in rote memory; he loses track of time when he is concentrating, he is a poor listener in class...but not in conversation, he is disorganized with school materials, and he is sometimes impulsive.

"See how much this list tells us about who Adam really is — not just his last name and what family he's from — but who Adam is, himself. You've done a thorough, loving job, and his patterns have been consistent since early childhood.

"These qualities are very different from yours, and it seems to me you've been more frightened by the difference than by the qualities themselves.

"It's so easy to see what kids AREN'T doing — or what they're doing wrong — that we sometimes forget to look for propensities. We need to notice interests and find ways to nourish them. Unexercised talents itch.

"Be a little easy on yourselves, too. In spite of your many differences, you and Adam share similar, strong human values. I know who it was who put a stop to the hazing in the locker room."

Willingness: "I know how we could get that effect."

At a planning meeting, Angela, the sixth grade class President said, "The play is going to include kids from each grade. That's a lot of kids! Our stage is just average size, so we've got a problem. Everybody's going to just look all jammed in."

"I know how we could get that effect. If we used different colors and shapes and levels, we would get that illusion. You know...a couple of kindergarten chairs down front, on one side a bench from a cafeteria table at an angle, a science lab stool in the back corner...and then big cardboard boxes — some painted dark, some bright. Once I built a..." Adam looked around, wondering where the voice had come from. He had not intended to say a word.

* * *

"Janet and Walt, thank you for coming in to school with Adam. We need to hammer out some plans."

"OK," Adam said, "I want to make the stage set, but not if everybody's going to bug me."

"Adam, it won't work unless you make some drawings first."

"Dad, that's just what I mean. I get an idea, and now you're telling me how to carry it out. I KNOW how, and I don't need to draw it. You're just as bad as my math teacher: write it down. I don't need to, and I won't do it."

"Adam, this meeting is for cooperation — what everybody WILL do. Let's see what you're willing to promise, and what commitments your parents are willing to make. How about it? Walt? Janet? Can you pick Adam up by car the days he stays late to work on the project? Good. Can you excuse him from household chores the nights he gets he gets home late, so he can have time to finish his homework? Good. Adam, can you be ready and waiting when your Dad gets here to pick you up? And, you understand your obligation to keep up-to-date on your work? I'll see if some of your teachers will shorten their assignments for the duration of the project.

"I think we all need to agree that this is Adam's project. Help is available if he needs it, but it's his idea so it's his responsibility."

"Agreed."

"What if it doesn't work?"

"That's Adam's chance and Adam's choice. He knows where to find help if he wants it. Adults need to know when to let go."

* * *

"Adam, Mrs. Debeny says you've made a wonderful optical illusion. At rehearsals, the stage seems big enough to hold an army. Things are going so well! You're doing better in all your subjects, and you haven't 'lost' your homework since you first went to work on this project."

"I know. School is better this year. Mr. Tripp was right. I don't mind doing the work if it's fun."

"You've grown up a lot, Adam. Give yourself some credit. You think a lot of things are fun now. Before it just used to be the easy, goof-off stuff. By the way, what did you decide about the finale for the show? You said the song is great, but you need some sort of visual punch line?"

"It's still a problem. The ending is nice enough...but it doesn't have any kick. I don't know how to jet it. I haven't got it, yet."

"You want help? OK. It's your show. You'll figure it out."

Accord: "Adam did it."

The children sang the finale, their hands hidden behind their backs. At the last chord, all the players pulled forward their paper-bag masks, and, as the music played a coda, they slipped the bags over their heads. Color! Energy! Originality!

They had each chosen what their masks would look like — different kinds of bright colors and faces. They were all characters from one story on the stage together, but each was an individual.

As the audience clapped and the junior performers took their bows, cameras clicked, and the youngest member of the cast lost his professional detachment and waved to his mother. The small stage actually looked like a big space, and the riot of color was like a vivid summer garden.

Mrs. Debeny came out from behind the set and thanked the parents for their help with costumes and rehearsal schedules, and for being such a fine audience. Then, she said, "We have another very special person to thank. Come out here, Adam. Everyone needs a chance to clap for what you've made, and what you've helped the players make."

Walt squeezed Janet's hand. "Remember?"

"How could I forget?"

"The best thing is, we didn't make this happen...we let it happen. Adam did it."

Adam wasn't particularly big for 12, but he stood tall for the applause.

* * *

"Great job."

"We're very proud."

Rekindled affection and new-found mutual respect fired the warmth of his parents' congratulations, and the readiness of Adam's response.

"Thanks, Dad. Thanks, Mom. Hey, how did you like it at the end, when all the kids put on their different paper-bag masks?"

"We liked it very much! It wouldn't have been a very interesting story if everyone had been the same."

"And, by the way, it's great to hear you whistle."

AFTERWORD

Emotion is the On/Off switch for learning. Feeding into this switch are those lines or cables which carry the current. To function safely and effectively, they must be insulated so as not to scorch their surroundings, free of knots, and protected from potential damage by water, frost, fire, or overexposure to hostile elements.

These wires might be likened to the experiences and teaching which come to the child. When they are free of kinks, in good repair, and safe to use, emotion turns the switch to On.

When fed by power, the refrigerator keeps food fresh and moist, the electric stove cooks it so it is both palatable and nourishing, the lighted lamps make rooms hospitable, the furnace produces warmth, the stack of little black boxes gives forth music, and the water heater makes it possible to have a hot bath or shower. Zones converge. Life hums. This is a model of the learning child: sensing, planning, pondering, enjoying, and using the machinery at hand to make the most of the moment.

Anger, reluctance, dehumanization, frustration, perplexity, loneliness, and fear are some of the emotions which turn the switch to Off. Then, the power from the source doesn't reach the appliances. The refrigerator is warm, the stove cold, the lamps dark, the furnace still, the radio silent, the water heater dormant.

The learner stumbles around in the dark, feeling for familiar landmarks, with luck locating a spare blanket, a package of Graham Crackers, and taking a sip of water from the faucet. While these will keep freezing and starvation at bay, they are grim, survival-level supports and a far cry from coziness, hospitality, nourishment, and that safety which, paradoxically, encourages risk.

Because we are human, all children — and their parents and teachers — will from time to time experience the negative emotions which turn the switch to Off, creating dark, chilly, thirsty, hungry times. This is the price tag for the ambiguity of human nature.

But, for the most part, enlightened encouragement and exposure to positive experiences can help young learners develop and sustain realistic, optimistic expectations, and

Gather Power
Charge Energies
Diminish Negatives
Enhance Positives
Focus Potential
Reach Out
Tap Resources

and

Switch On.

RESOURCE SECTION

Five Organizations

Modern Learning Press/Programs for Education, Box 167, Rosemont, NJ 08556 (1-800-627-5867). This excellent publishing house offers a wide variety of wholly reliable, exciting materials for educators and parents. They are a welcome resource.

Educators Publishing Service, 75 Moulton St., Cambridge, MA 02138. This publisher offers materials originally designed for dyslexics which work magnificently in regular classrooms. The descriptions and age/grade levels in their catalogues are scrupulously fair.

The Orton Dyslexia Society, Chester Building, Suite 382, 8600 LaSalle Rd., Baltimore, MD 21204-6020. This organization brings together physicians, researchers, educators, and parents, offering excellent publications and conferences open to any interested participant.

The Coalition of Essential Schools, Box 1969, Brown University, Providence, RI 02912. This organization, run by Theodore Sizer, is a major recipient of the Annenberg $500 million dollar gift for research and enlightened practice in American education. For the past several years, the Coalition has published a small journal named *Horace*, available for a small fee to interested people.

CLASS (Center on Learning, Assessment and School Structure), Geneseo, NY. This is the brainchild of Grant Wiggins, whose book, *Assessing Student Performance: Exploring the Purpose and Limit of Testing* (in press at this writing), stands to make a major contribution to students' joy in learning, through structuring measures of mastery to display competence rather than find out failings.

General Bibliography

Priscilla Vail's books
(available at bookstores or from Modern Learning Press — see above)

About Dyslexia: Unraveling the Myth. Rosemont, NJ: Modern Learning Press/Programs for Education, 1990.

Clear & Lively Writing: Language Games and Activities for Everyone. New York: Walker & Co., 1981.

Common Ground: Whole Language and Phonics Working Together. Rosemont, NJ: Modern Learning Press/ Programs for Education, 1991.

Gifted, Precocious, or Just Plain Smart. Rosemont, NJ: Modern Learning Press/ Programs for Education, 1987.

Learning Styles: Food for Thought and 130 Practical Tips. Rosemont, NJ: Modern Learning Press/Programs for Education, 1992.

Smart Kids With School Problems: Things to Know and Ways to Help. New York: NAL Plume Paperback, 1989.

The World of the Gifted Child. New York: Walker & Co., 1979 (currently between printings, available through libraries).

Other Authors and Titles

Cohen, Alfie. *No Contest: The Case Against Competition.* Boston: Houghton Mifflin, 1992. This is the manual for cooperative learning, which — with humor and wisdom — lays out the reasons for cooperation and the practices which foster it.

Cziksmentmihali, Mihaly. *The Evolving Self: A Psychology for the Third Millenium*. New York : Harper Collins, 1993. In this sequel to *Flow: The Psychology of Optimal Experience*, the author says, "Perhaps the most urgent task facing us is to create a new educational curriculum that will make each child aware, from 1st grade on, that life in the universe is interdependent. It should be an education that trains the mind to perceive the network of causes and effects in which our actions are embedded, and trains the emotions and the imagination to respond appropriately to the consequences of those actions." as excerpted in Education Week, Dec. 1, 1993)

Gardner, Howard. *Frames of Mind: the Theory of Multiple Intelligences*. New York: Basic Books, 1984. In this barrier-breaking book, Gardner expands the number and precision of the lenses through which we assess intelligence and recognize the potential in the children among us.

Gardner, Howard. *The Unschooled Mind: How Children Think and How Schools Should Teach Them*. New York: Basic Books, 1992. Gardner gives us an insightful tour of the mind of the 5-year-old thinker alive in all of us, and suggests ways to help learners move beyond that primitive level to genuine understanding.

Gardner, Howard. *Multiple Intelligences: The Theory in Practice*. New York: Basic Books, 1993. The title of this volume speaks for its contents. Although hefty and sometimes cumbersome, it fills a need.

Grant, Jim. *I Hate School!* Rosemont, NJ: Modern Learning Press/Programs for Education, 1986. This is a guide to the feelings and experiences of overplaced students.

Hallowell, Edward M. and Thompson, Michael G. *Finding the Heart of the Child.* Braintree, MA: Association of Independent Schools of Massachusetts, 1993. As I said in my jacket blurb, "This book is Araidne's thread through the labyrinths of human emotions and needs. The reader can trust the two author/guides who laid this thread through a maze, to the very center, and back out again. Delicate and strong, questioning and answering, this collection of essays offers insights to its readers, solace to its subjects, and delight to those who care about both people and prose."

Hallowell, Edward M. and Ratey, John J. *Driven to Distraction: Attention Deficit Disorder in Children and Adults.* New York: Pantheon Books, 1994. This barrier-breaking book cuts away the confusion surrounding ADD/ADHD, as it offers practical advice and encouragement. A must for anyone who cares about kids (and people of other ages, too).

deHirsch, Katrina. *Language and the Developing Child.* Baltimore: the Orton Dyslexia Society, Monograph #4, 1984. This is a scholarly guide to the structures of language which go hand-in-hand with learning and emotion in the developing child.

Healy, Jane M. *Your Child's Growing Mind.* New York: Doubleday, 1987. This well researched, solid, entertaining book lays strong foundations for understanding children's learning.

Healy, Jane M. *Endangered Minds.* New York: Doubleday, 1989. This book explores ways our current culture may be altering not only how children think, but their brains as well.

Henry, Marcia. *Words*. Lex Press, Box 859, Los Gatos, CA 95031. Dr. Henry's materials focus on word origins, roots and affixes. Students enjoy using them; teachers find them clear and successful.

Katz, Lillian. *Engaging Children's Minds: The Project Approach*. Norwood, NJ: Ablex Publishers, 355 Chestnut St., 07648. Practical, sensitive, and experienced, Katz continually couples children's learning with children's feelings. She's on target again.

Restak, Richard, *The Brain*. New York: Bantam Books, 1984. An incredible resource for the lay person.

Restak, Richard, *The Mind*. New York: Bantam Books, 1988. Again, this scientist and physician leads us to and through the complexities of what is known so far about the human mind.

Restak, Richard. *The Brain Has a Mind of Its Own*. New York: Crown, 1991. Compatible with some of the most sophisticated investigations going on now, this book helps the lay person see the connection between mind and brain.

Schafer, Edith N. *Our Remarkable Memory*. Washington and Philadelphia: Starrhill Press, 1988. This tiny volume contains wisdom, exquisitely precise and reliable information, and humor. Schafer renders complicated material accessible to the lay person in 75 pages. A stellar achievement!

Seligman, Martin, E.P. *Helplessness: on Depression, Development, and Death*. San Francisco: W.H. Freeman & Co., 1975. Here we find the earliest descriptions of "learned helplessness," its causes, manifestations, and ways to jolt it into submission.

Seligman, Martin E.P. *Learned Optimism*. New York: Knopf, 1991. In this sequel, Seligman shows us how "explanatory style" both underlies and directs our thinking.

Sizer, Theodore R. *Horace's School*. Boston: Houghton Mifflin Co., 1992. This practical, philosophically wise, and dazzlingly original book shows us how and where to go to put learning back in education.

Turecki, Stanley. *Emotional Problems of Normal Children*. New York: Bantam, 1994. This book, by the author of *The Difficult Child*, delivers the promise implied in the title and offers practical suggestions for daily living.

Zingler, Gary. *At the Pirate Academy: Adventures with Language In the Library Media Center*. Chicago, London: ALA 1990. This book recounts the experiences of a library/media center teacher and his highly successful ways of bringing focused creativity into all aspects of school life. Practical, original, and humorous, it is an educator's very good friend!

Source Notes & References By Chapter

Chapter 1
#1 Restak, *The Brain*. p. 136.
#2 LeDoux, *New York Times*, July 15, 1989.
#3 Sizer, *Horace's School*, p. 143.
#4 Bryan, Tanis & Bryan, Jas. *Journal of Learning Disabilities*, vol. 24, #8, October, 1991.
#5 convergent zones: *New York Times*, Sept. 10, 1991, also *Scientific American Special Issue: Mind and Brain*, Sept. 1992, also Kinoshita, Mapping the Mind, *New York Times Magazine*, Oct. 18, 1992.
#6 Hallowell, *Finding the Heart of the Child*, essay on Connectedness.

#7 Gould, Stephen Jay, *New York Times*, July 30, 1989.
#8 Sizer, *Horace's School*, p. 26.

Chapter 2
#1 Seligman, *Learned Optimism*.
#2 Angell, Roger, *The New Yorker*, double issue Dec. 28, 1992 and Jan. 4, 1993.
Books
Hoban, Russell. *How Tom Beat Captain Najork and His Hired Sportsmen*. New York: Atheneum, 1974.
Werner, Emmy E., and Sith, Ruth S. *Overcoming the Odds*. Cornell University Press, 1992.
Articles
Priscilla's Column, *New York Orton Dyslexia Society Newsletter*: The Pony, May, 1983 and Daphne and the Butterflies, August 1985.
Education Week, June 9, 1993

Chapter 3
#1 Kagan, Jerome. The Shy and the Sociable: Antecedents of Introversion and Extroversion, *Harvard Medical Magazine*, Winter 1990/1991, and The Nature of Shyness, *Harvard Magazine*, March/April, 1992.
#2 Hallowell, *Finding the Heart of the Child*.
Articles
Angier, Natalie. The Purpose of Playful Frolics: Training for Adulthood, *New York Times*, Oct. 20, 1992.
Sexson, Sandra B., and Madan-Swain, Avi. School Reentry for the Child With Chronic Illness, *Journal of Learning Disabilities*, vol. 26, #2, Feb., 1993.

Chapter 4
See General Bibliography

Chapter 5
Books
Levine, Mel. *Keeping A Head in School*. Cambridge: Educator's Publishing Co., 1990.

Secunda, Victoria. *Women and Their Fathers: The Sexual and Romantic Impact of the First Man in Your Life*. New York : Delacorte Press, 1992.

Articles
Baldwin, Bruce. Cornucopia Kids. *Brown University Family Therapy Letter*, Aug. 1991.

Katz, Lillian. Reading, Writing, and Narcissism, *New York Times*, July 15, 1993.

Kutner, Lawrence. Remember, It's the Child's Life or Should Be: the pressure of having too many fun things to do, *New York Times*, Nov. 5, 1992.

An Organization
National Outdoor Leadership School, Lander, WY.

Chapter 6
#1, #2, #3 Goleman, Daniel. Study of Play Yields Clues to Success, *New York Times*, October 2, 1990.

#4 Kutner, L. Bullying: A Test of the Limits of One's Power and Control, *New York Times*, Oct. 28, 1993.

#5 Mary. *How Does Your Garden Grow*. Providence, RI: Mary, Inc. 72 Waterman St., 1973.

Chapter 7
#1 Jones, Waldo B. Report on results of a study funded by the Moore Foundation on The Role of School in Children's Lives, 1983.

Chapter 8
Books
Feldman, David Henry. *Nature's Gambit*. New York: Basic Books, 1986.

Renzulli, Joseph S., and Reis, Sally M. *The Schoolwide Enrichment Model*. Mansfield Center, CT: Creative Learning Press, Inc., 1993.

Sternberg, Robert. *Beyond I.Q.: A Triarchic Theory of Human Intelligence*. New York: Cambridge University Press, 1987.

INDEX

H

Hallowell, Edward 85
hearing 62, 63, 98, 100
humor 42, 54, 75–76, 80, 162, 175, 223–224

I

illness 61–64
intellect 7, 15, 19, 59, 66
intelligence 15, 52, 153, 195, 218–219, 225

J

joy 21, 22, 45, 49, 85, 159

K

Kaufman, Alan 218, 219

L

language 3, 11, 17, 18, 81, 108, 182, 185–186, 190–193, 198, 204
learning 1, 30, 35, 44, 49, 58, 60, 72–79, 87, 91, 106, 112, 123,
   130–131, 138, 140, 146, 155–156, 161, 165, 172, 182, 186,
   188, 194–195, 198, 204–205, 209, 214, 219, 220, 222
learning disabilities 183, 219
Levine, Mel 67, 148
limbic system 2, 3, 4, 59, 201, 207
locus of control 9, 36, 70
loneliness 55, 59, 119, 137, 140, 151, 166–167, 169, 171
love 53, 94, 113, 119–151, 182, 213, 216

M

mathematics 125, 127, 189, 202, 220
music 65, 96, 125

O

organization 67, 188, 192, 199–200
overplacement 72, 162

P

parents 106, 131, 138, 151, 198
perplexity 137–138, 140, 151
poetry 23, 108, 146, 204
portfolios 22–23
pride 22, 121, 202, 205, 215–217, 224
proclivities 221

R

rejection 134
reluctance 57–86, 138, 191, 214